UrbAn

About the Authors

Raven Kaldera

is a Neopagan shaman, homesteader, activist, musician, astrologer, and wordsmith who did time in many cities before escaping. If you want to know more, do a Web search on his name.

" 'Tis an ill wind that blows no minds."

Tannin Schwartzstein

has dedicated a significant part of her life to the pursuit of the spiritual arts, both privately and professionally. Tannin has studied diverse practices and paths, such as chi gong, shamanistic energy techniques, gnosticism, Afro-Caribbean religions, and even a pinch of ceremonial magic. She is the proprietor of Bones and Flowers, Worcester's (Massachusetts) only occult specialty store (www.bonesandflowers.com), a crafter in diverse media (acrylics, small sculpture, ceramic, bone, wood, etc.), and a legally ordained Pagan minister.

The Urban Primitive

Raven Kaldera &
Tannin Schwartzstein

Paganism in the Concrete Jungle

2002
Llewellyn Publications
St. Paul, Minnesota 55164-0383, U.S.A.

FIRST EDITION
First Printing, 2002

Book design and editing by Rebecca Zins
Cover photo © Arthur Tress/Photonica
Cover design by Lisa Novak
Interior illustrations by W. Michael (Wolfie) Dooley and Sean Petrin

Library of Congress Cataloging-in-Publication Data
Kaldera, Raven.
The urban primitive : paganism in the concrete jungle / Raven Kaldera & Tannin Schwartzstein.—1st ed.
p. cm.
Includes bibliographical references and index.
ISBN 0-7387-0259-5
1. Magic. 2. Cities and towns—Miscellanea. 3. Neopaganism. 4. City dwellers—Religious life. 5. Cities and towns—Religious aspects—Neopaganism. I. Schwartzstein, Tannin. II. Title.

BF1623.C5 K33 2002
299—dc21

2002069501

Llewellyn Publications
A Division of Llewellyn Worldwide, Ltd.
P.O. Box 64383, Dept. 0-7387-0259-5
St. Paul, MN 55164-0383, U.S.A.
www.llewellyn.com

Printed in the United States of America

thanks to . . .

Beth Harper, Toni, Shelley, JB Dreamweaver, and all the great people on the Pagan Homeschoolers Email Support Group who told us about their urban experiences and allowed us to get to know the magic of cities we'd never seen.

Joan, for her helpful suggestions about city survival, and to Bella, the herbalist, for her plant identification and for believing in us, and to MagicRat the cyberwalker for her inspired poetry. Special thanks to Sean and Wolfie, our illustrators, for giving vision to our voices.

This book is dedicated
in loving memory of John Kuziemko,
Urban Pagan and good friend.

It's choosing your own blessed face,
Wearing it with grace,
Carving out a place
There on the edge,
Thin end of a wedge,
Getting out of the rat race, let me tell you,
Is digging the Whole before the cat smells you . . .

MagicRat, 1999

Contents

Introduction: The Urban Primitive

When Tannin was nineteen years old, she was fresh out of suburbia and had recently moved into Worcester, the second largest city in Massachusetts. At the end of her first year of college, she attended a large gathering outside of New York City; a circle at a camp retreat. During the course of the weekend there were many different discussion groups, and one of them was about energy. One of the facilitators kept praising the energy of the forest—and mind you, this was not a real forest in any sense of the word, it was just a suburban camp with patchy trees and trailer hookups. She praised it for its peace, beauty, and tranquility, and expressed a desire to move out of the cold, dead city.

Tannin wondered if she was crazy. Although she could understand not liking the place, the energy of the city that she'd experienced her first few months after arriving was anything but cold and dead. Aside from meeting tons of other practitioners from other walks of life, she had run headlong into a world of ghosts and spirits, and a sea of thick, chaotic, noisy (if somewhat impersonal) energy. Since then, she has continued to grow and mature in this concrete womb—and she calls it that because it's insular; no matter how big a city is, you never realize how strong its boundaries are until you leave. Tannin's city—Worcester, Massachusetts—is sometimes her friend, sometimes her adversary, but she always comes back to him.

One of the things that makes us giggle about the modern Neo-pagan movement is that although there are a lot of good psychological and practical reasons to make contact with our rural and agricultural roots, modern Neopaganism is primarily an urban movement. Most Pagans, and especially the new generation of young Pagans, live in urban areas. There are more resources in cities for Pagans, a higher likelihood of finding others to practice with, and it is easier to blend in and hide, if that's what you want. Those of us who practice real urban magic are trying to see beyond the rote, brutal mundanity of twenty-first-century urban life to something deeper, and those of us who are lower income may live a life that is startlingly close in many ways to that of our more "primitive" hunter-gatherer ancestors.

However, unlike those ancestors who lived a "healthy outdoor lifestyle," we have become isolated from the rest of the circle of life. The average hunter-gatherer may have only known about thirty other humans intimately, and only seen members of other tribes about once a month (to whom he probably reacted with hostility, which makes him not that different from we city dwellers when someone invades our circle), but he felt intimately surrounded by a host of other spirits: the cougar, the bear, the deer, the oak tree, the river, and so on. The fact is that cities do pollute the Earth. They are boils upon the ass of Gaea, and there's no getting around that fact. They devour more than they return to Her, from every soda can to every paper mill. We should not attempt to romanticize what is a real problem, but there are many of us who believe that something ought to be done, although we aren't sure what it is. We do feel that abandoning the cities is not the answer, and so the urban tribes are gathering.

It is a mistake to assume that cities are a modern phenomenon. The ancient world had many famous cities, from Thebes in Egypt to Ur in Sumeria to Athens in Greece, and their populace was no less urban than that of San Francisco or New York. In fact, as cities grew up around great temples, many of the earliest recorded Pagan religious writings were created and preserved in places like Jerusalem, Alexandria, and Rome. Most purely hunter-gatherer or agricultural societies had little writing, and little time to do it in. Much of what we know about those societies comes from the written observations of urbane, and urban, ancient Pagans.

A friend of Tannin's once said, in reference to evolving musical styles, "The more civilized we get, the more primitive we become." One could easily apply this statement to urban life. By "primitive" we mean not dull but *primal*, that which was there first. As we use our technology to get rid of more and more of the discomforts of being human, the more those vulnerable, emotional, mortal aspects of ourselves come to the forefront.

Often we wonder if, through this thing we call modern Paganism, we are trying to look back through our history and see if we missed something. Much writing on the subject seems to be a desperate search for "where it all went wrong." This is not to say at all that it's solved—far from it—but now we've ended up with a new breed of urban primitive who are sticking bits of metal through their noses, and talking to buildings as if they were trees, and finding, inexplicably, that it helps to settle the burning in their brains.

The city Pagan comes in many shapes, sizes, and incarnations. She may be a leather-jacketed warrior with multiple tattoos and piercings, or a soccer mom with three kids who shields her tiny apartment with scattered Rice Krispies. He may be a biker Pagan who lives a twentieth-century tribal lifestyle, or a youth who is tired of the poor role models offered to him and sees redemption and meaning in such figures as Herne the Hunter or Zeus the Competent Leader. There are teenyboppers who are looking for something more interesting to do than watching *Buffy the Vampire Slayer*—they want more than just to see magic, they want to *be* the magic as well. Some urban goddess-worshippers cling to Gaea as a surrogate mother, both attempting to heal childhoods of poor nurturing and striving to touch the deeper power within them.

This book is written for all of you, for everyone who loves the city they live in and doesn't want to feel guilty about it . . . and those of you who are just trying to cope. It's especially for those of you who are struggling without a lot of money or resources, who barely had the spare change to buy this book. We've been where you are, and we understand. Our hearts go out to you, and we hope that this little spellbook can help make your existence easier. In these pages you'll find ways to forage for supplies, evade predators, forge tribal alliances, and seek the blessings of old gods in new guises. Enjoy!

City Witch Song

In the long ago and the far away
We tilled the soil and worked the clay
We danced the cycle from day to day . . .
We walked in the patterns of moon and sun
The Earth's deep rhythm in our blood would run
'til the foul wind swept it away . . .

Many long years have passed since then
And the circle song now rises again
And we must choose as we crouch in the ruins of men . . .
To turn our hearts toward the last deep green,
At the cost of pity to follow the dream
Or to lend the help of our hands.

Chorus

I'm a witch in the cave of the city's tomb,
I weave my web on a high steel loom,
And a new power grows in this cold stone womb;
To heal the wounds of the masses lost,
We're the generation that carries the cost
Of averting humanity's doom.

But the Mother's land is split and sold
And the Green Man's peace must be bought with gold
And millions banished to the cities cold . . .
If the work of the witch is the work of change
Then our greatest task is to break those chains
That cost so many their souls.

So we bruise our hearts on these concrete cairns
And we lose our voice in the caustic air
Though at times it seems too much to bear . . .
Can we turn our backs on this terrible cry—
Going back to the land is a privilege high
And the gods ask: How much can you care?

Chorus

I'm a witch in the cave of the city's tomb,
I weave my web on a high steel loom,
And a new power grows in this cold stone womb;
To heal the wounds of the masses lost,
We're the generation that carries the cost
Of averting humanity's doom.

Bridge

So we forge each link,
With hearts and arms and telephone wire,
And we win each step
A little further from the funeral pyre,
And we hold on tight,
And we drag each other up out of the mire,
And we weave our web
Until we close humanity in;
For nothing yet invented
Can truly quench this fire.

So listen my children, let me tell you clear,
Why we have wheels but we're still here;
Where there's fear there's power;
Where there's change there's fear;
To the cries of the city we raise our voice,
A living example that there is a choice,
To the lost a candle,
To the hopeless a star,
To the walking dead a mirror.

Chorus

I'm a witch in the cave of the city's tomb,
I weave my web on a high steel loom,
And a new power grows in this cold stone womb;
To heal the wounds of the masses lost,
We're the generation that carries the cost
Of averting humanity's doom. . . .

Raven Kaldera, 1994

one

Lay of the Land

THE ENERGY OF THE CITY

• • Most Pagan rituals, spells, and symbols stem from an older, agricultural era. The holidays follow the Wheel of the Year as seen by farmers dependent on it for their food; the rituals revolve around fertility and growing things. This is a difficult path for many city dwellers to follow, surrounded as they are by the energy of a different place and time.

Seasons pass differently in the city; although climatic changes are the same, there are less natural cues, short of the weather, to notice. Even moon cycles are harder to follow in the city. There is more obscuring light pollution, and tall buildings may block the moon when she is hanging lower in the sky.

Granted, it is important to know your roots, to connect with your ancestral patterns, and above all to understand where your food comes from. One thing that is artificial about living in a city is that the majority of food production necessarily happens far away, and urban dwellers are quite dependent on their rural neighbors for almost everything they put in their mouths. This connection is vital, and should be appreciated, and to that end we encourage all city dwellers to periodically take time away from the urban centers in order to connect with the spirit of the giving Earth. Find a farm, and pick apples or help cut cabbages. Acknowledge how dependent you are on rural people for your living, and be respectful of this.

On the other hand, the city has special energies all its own. First, there is so very much energy in a city, floating around everywhere, far more than in most rural places, where it's more spread out or peaceful. The city is really a wild place, with much more in common with the unsettled wilderness than the tamed farmland. Most rural energy is that of growing things—it's tame, agricultural, in cooperation with humankind. Just as the gods of the deep woods and thick swamps are much wilder than the gods of the fields, the city gods are wild creatures as well, with the swamp of urban energy swirling around like a whirlpool, like quicksand, like a vortex. And one should never live in a place for very long and not seek out and make a working relationship with the god/desses of that place. It's important to do this.

The energy in a city, no matter what its size, is thick and soupy. People who live in a rural area may still create psychic pollution, but there are more natural filters, such as trees, rivers, and verdure, to absorb and transform it. Since concrete doesn't ground energy well, the psychic pollution in a city tends to "bounce" and stay in the atmosphere. As you move about a city, you may feel overwhelmed by the great waves of energy that are washing over you; it's like being in the ocean for the first time. Instead of fighting against the undertow, try to let yourself float about in it, like a cork on the surface of the sea.

One reason that there is so much uncontrolled energy in a city is the sheer number of people who live there and radiate their feelings and needs into the morass. There are more large, living creatures packed into less square footage in the cities than in the country;

most of them simply happen to be human animals. The density of their combined auras creates a massive, smothering blanket of thinking, reasoning, feeling, hysterical energy. If you live in that city, you are a part of that mass aura, whether you realize it or not. You can learn to tap into this vortex and feel out how the general temperament of the city is doing.

More people die in cities, too, because of the population, the crime rate, and the multitude of hospitals. This means the ghosts are much thicker in urban areas than in rural or suburban ones. Many of these ghosts will choose to stay around. You may find them still haunting their old areas, or they may have been sucked into the vortex that is the "spirit of the city." Yes, each city has its own guardian spirit, one whose character is shaped by the souls of its living and dead. The specific spirit of each city has a personality all its own; this internal nature may change over time, but it will be very slow to alter, as various groups and cultures of people may enter or flee. It will reflect the major attitudes and opinions of the population, including class differences, celebrations, depressions, poverty, and riches. Things that may change a city spirit's nature over time are massive influxes of immigrants from foreign cultures, or the growth of new industries.

City spirits are, not surprisingly, quite social creatures, and they love to be acknowledged, so it's worth your while to learn to speak to them. It may take a while at first; they have a lot to do and many voices to listen to, and you're only one voice among many, but keep talking to them and they will eventually hear you and answer. After that, expect them to drop by quite frequently for psychic coffee and donuts, so to speak. They may also become possessive of you, and try to prevent you from moving away from them. You may actually want to hold off on contacting the city spirit if you intend to be leaving soon.

To introduce yourself to the city spirit, you'll need to find the "heart" of the city, or its strongest location. The heart of the city isn't necessarily where the city planners, or selectmen, or advertisers, or even neighborhood dwellers may tell you that it is. In very large and complex cities, such as New York, each borough may have its own heart, and then a central heart above and beyond that (for example, New York's overall heart is located somewhere in Manhattan).

You might start by looking for a common, or the place where a common was when the city was founded. Anywhere that people gather almost automatically, instinctively, is a likely culprit. Look for busy parks, or the oldest building in a city. Sometimes the heart is so obvious that everybody knows where it is and can tell you—for example, the pit in the center of Harvard Square is the heart of Cambridge. Other times it may be more nebulous. Like a human heart where blood flows in and out again continuously, the heart of a city will be the place where the energy flows in and out the quickest.

When you've found it, if it has a predominant structure such as a statue or building, lean up against it. Sit on the step. In your mind, introduce yourself and ask it how it's doing. Cities love the question, "What's going on?" because their answer is always "Me."

After you've made contact, sit quietly and breathe. Look around you and watch everything. Imagine that you are a living video camera, recording an image in your mind of everything that is going on around the city's heart. Once you've contacted the city spirit and exchanged pleasantries, you'll be able to talk to it anywhere inside city limits. You should periodically make offerings to it, and one of the most appropriate offerings is some food and drink that is traditional to the area. This might be, for example, Mexican food in San Antonio, Texas, or Italian food in Long Branch, New Jersey.

Another source of power is the power. There is more electrical energy in a city; we live surrounded by a web of power lines and grids that we take for granted. Contrary to what you might think, electricity isn't "mundane" energy, as opposed to mana/prana/chi/ki or whatever you choose to call "psychic," invisible energy. Energy is energy, whatever its form, and will affect you in some way. It's now being discovered that people who live right next to power stations have a whole slew of health problems. The steel web that surrounds city dwellers does affect them—perhaps not as drastically, but on some level they are absorbing those vibrations, for good or ill.

Because of this, the first order of business for any city dweller is protection, both from physical and from psychic difficulties. In chapter 3, Defenses, we will cover this information in depth. Protection from physical predators is an obvious need; it's easy to grasp the fear of muggers in dark alleys. But city dwellers need just as much to protect themselves from the constant swirl and fog of energy that billows and throbs in great glittering invisible clouds all around them. Effects of being immersed in that energy all the time range from fatigue to forgetfulness to depression. It's as if your third eye is constantly exposed to a strobe light, with the resulting dull headache. You need to be able to escape from the city's energy vortex, for your own health.

However, that same vortex can be useful as a source of power, if you know how to draw off it without hurting yourself. This is easier said than done, and requires careful practice, but one thing you won't have to worry about is using it up. There's more than enough for dozens of sorcerers in the average large urban sprawl. Once you learn how, you can tap into the whirl of power and draw off small amounts to use as workings.

What you will have to worry about is your health. If you take a glass tube and pour sewer water through it on a daily basis, after a while it will acquire a grimy residue and an unpleasant smell. If you do it long enough, it might even become permanently stained and discolored. Tiny scratches may develop on the inside, which catch filth and hold it. Eventually, it will become so disgusting that you'll want to discard it for a new one. This is a pretty close metaphor of what will happen to you if you channel the energy of the city on a regular basis and don't do periodic cleansing magics. Although those who are meant to live in the city will eventually develop something of a tolerance, it's best to be safe. Purification is especially important to city magicians. A magic-worker living in the country can go for a walk close to nature every couple of days and find themselves rejuvenated, but in some areas of the city, stepping outside your door may contribute to, rather than help, the problem. We'll discuss cleansing magics in chapter 4, Internal Hygiene.

This aforementioned sewer water problem is also why the city's vortex shouldn't be used as a source of vital energy. Don't try to use it to live on. After a while, you couldn't do enough purification rituals to keep up with the contamination. Urban energy should be used more like a tool than as food. Take it, channel it for a task, and then go clean up. Treat it as if you were using useful chemicals for a task: don't eat it, wash your hands afterwards, and don't leave a mess for someone else to step in later.

On the other hand, there are good points to utilizing urban energy. For instance, it tends to be very unfussy and nonjudgmental. This is not to say that some of the city's denizens might not judge you or be prejudiced against you, but as long as you're contributing, the city does not care.

The urban spirit's energy is so noisy and cantankerous that it's hard for one single person to disrupt it. Whatever kind of magic you may do—Christian, Pagan, Yoruba, Satanic—simply gets added to the morass without a blink. It's good for people who need a lot of stimulation, and for people whose energy is just plain noisy and likely to disturb others. In these cases, the city's blanket is so thick and strong that it will naturally flatten out and condense their auras with time and wear. It's also easier for people who "stand out" psychically to actually have a chance to blend in and learn stealth.

If you're especially sensitive, you will have to develop strong shields and learn how to handle those swirling crosscurrents more skillfully in order to keep from being overwhelmed. Although not everyone can handle this (and if you can't, you should probably get out), developing psychic "callouses" can be very useful training.

Another useful city benefit is that there are often big "happenings" that are major sources of freely given, fresh energy, such as concerts, ball games, festivals, block parties, ethnic celebrations, and parades. People who are natural psychic vampires often need more energy than they can ethically achieve in the country or suburbs, and are attracted to urban overpopulation for this reason. However, as any public speaker will tell you, riding the energy of a crowd and harnessing it to your needs is a risky thing at best. When a lot of people get together, the mood is often like a wild thing, and the energy can go any way.

Living on wild city energy is life in the fast lane. You can do it, but make sure that you have a hole to crawl into when you're tired out, and space to clean up in. Use moderation in all things. And above all, remember that the city is not everything. Urban dwellers often forget that theirs is not the only experience; that there is life outside the urban areas that demands respect, and indeed is where we all came from. Love your city, but get out occasionally. Remember your roots, and keep that link to Gaea strong.

two

Initiation

The Straight Poop on Spellcasting

• • Spellcasting. It's easy, right? Wiggle your fingers, say the right words, and *poof*! You get what you want.

NOT.

Spellcasting. It's complicated and uncomfortable, right? You have to have everything from the proper set of thousand-dollar robes to the right stuff in your stomach to a pharmacopoeia of obnoxious, illegal herbs and (ugh!) dried animal bits from obscure third-world countries. You must spend hours chanting things in languages you don't understand on the exact right phase of the moon.

Sorry, wrong again. (Unless that kind of thing really turns you on.)

If you're already an experienced magical worker, please feel free to skip this chapter. If you're a beginner, please read this so that certain concepts don't confuse you.

Spellcasting, in its myriad of forms, boils down to the following: (1) the generation of energy, or "juice"; (2) the movement of that energy to where you want it to go (injecting the juice); and (3) the bounceback or ripples. Magic isn't like throwing a baseball at something. It's more like tying a wire to your body, attaching the other end to a harpoon, shooting the sucker into your goal, and then running current along it. The current will actually go back and forth several times between you and your stated object, affecting both of you.

Another metaphor might be likening a spell to injecting something intravenously into the circulatory system of the cosmos. Eventually it will make its way to the heart, and then to the "limb" that needs the effect. At the same time, since you're part of that circulatory system, it will affect you too. Frankly and honestly, the bounceback is how you know the spell worked. Even if (and we really don't recommend this) you are casting a rotten spell on someone else, if it doesn't come back in kind on you, it didn't affect them. You missed.

And sometimes you will miss. Sometimes you just won't have the focus or the juice to do it right. And also, sometimes the universe just says NO. Perhaps the problem was way, way bigger than you thought it was, so big that you alone can't fix it, no matter how much juice you throw at it. An example would be an attempt to cure someone of depression. There might be hundreds of factors—brain chemistry, an entire childhood of abuse or neglect, a lifetime of bad habits, alcohol or drug problems, allergies, a bad relationship, or too much of the wrong energy in their current apartment. One spell can't erase all of that, especially not in any timely fashion. Spellcasting is not wish magic. As every child learns, wishing doesn't make it so.

So what can we actually do? Well, to start with, spells create options. They give you more choices than you had. They can sometimes level a playing field, or slant it slightly in your direction, but you still have to get up and swing the bat and run around the bases. You can't work against your own magic. You can do magic to get a job, but you still have to go out and fill out applications and do interviews. Magic simply triggers opportunities—on your way out of the office from one interview, someone else says, "Hey, I think you should try over in that department!" Or, if we were to take our example of the individual with the depression problem, magic could be used to give them the courage and knowledge to start the healing process, whatever that might be . . . but they'd still have to see the shrink, take the meds, dump the boyfriend, face the fears, or whatever specific things were necessary to fix the problem. Magic does not get you out of doing work, it gives you what it takes to be able to do it.

Magic can be divided into two basic categories. (No, not black or white.) The first kind is magic that you do yourself, using your own juice. The jury's out as to whether that energy comes from you, from the universe through you, or whether these are just the same things anyway. It doesn't matter, because you won't need to know that in order to do it. Most of the spellworkings in this book are basic "personal energy" magic. Doing this competently is a technique that can be learned.

The other kind of magic is done by asking for help. This includes invoking elementals or deities and asking them for their aid. This second kind of magic should not be used unless you've already tried the first kind, which in turn should not be used unless nonmagical means have failed. Don't bribe the spirits to do your homework or shopping, and don't bother Athena with your petty little problems unless you're sure that you can't handle it yourself.

Sensing the Energy

The first step is to be able to come up with enough energy to do the job. If you're a beginner and you haven't had a lot of experience working with energy, you may want to prepare by doing some exercises that hone your abilities in sensing and gathering energy.

This is a simple and basic technique for sensing energy: Rub your hands together briskly for ten to twenty seconds. Pull them apart very slightly so that there is a small space between your palms and they are not actually touching. After a few seconds, the prickly feeling from the friction will wear off, and you should move your hands just a little further apart, about an inch. Do you feel any heat or cold or tingling with your palms, as if there is a pillow of something between them? As soon as you can feel that consistently, pull your hands further apart. When they're too far apart and it begins to fade, push them further together. Go back and forth, finding out where it is strongest and where it is weakest. It may feel like a push, forcing your hands apart, or a pull, bringing them closer together. Some people take to this technique immediately; others need several attempts, sometimes on separate days. If it isn't working, try again tomorrow.

Practice. Do it over and over. What you're aiming for is to be able to produce it without the rubbing, to know how it feels to have it well up, to know that so well that you can do it at will without rubbing your hands together. Eventually you should be able to hold your hands facing upward and create a controlled "pad" of energy on each one.

Now that you can create that little pad of energy between your hands, describe it. Does it have a color? What color is it? Is it watery or muddy or electric, slow or fast, push or pull? Does it come from your fingertips or from the centers of your hands? What part of your body does it seem to flow from—your heart, your belly, your head, or somewhere else? Can you mold it into various shapes, as if you were sculpting clay? If you can do this with a partner, try to pass them your energy object. It may change shape as they take it, which indicates that their conscious or unconscious mind influenced it, but they may be able to guess what it was when you had it.

The point of this baby exercise is that you can use this energy to charge physical objects such as candles, tools, and any old junk you might pick up and want to use in a spell. Practice makes perfect, and you will eventually be able to inject something with a small zorch of energy, as if you were the outlet and it was an appliance.

The Stuff of Spellcasting

When you think of spellcasting, you probably think of the props: the candles, the poppets, the knives, and so forth. These props are used for two reasons. First of all, the part of your mind that allows the energy to come forth isn't the part that understands negotiation, parking tickets, and the IRS. It's your right brain, your deep unconscious, part of your limbic system. Some people refer to it as your inner child, although that's both inaccurate and an oversimplification. Whatever it is, it doesn't do reasons. It may not even care about the goal of your spell, unless it's something you feel very emotional over. It needs to be wooed, seduced like a three-year-old. It likes colors, textures, drama, neat toys, and cool props to keep it focused. If you don't get on its good side, it'll shut off the flow, so half of any spell is dictated by that part of you. You communicate with it through feelings—What does this color feel like to you? This texture? This scent? This word?—and adjust appropriately.

On the other hand, it's not all in your head. Physical items do have "vibrations," energies that are integral and unique to themselves, and they will add their own specific energies to a spell. Sometimes these energies are gross and obvious—no one needs to be told that a chunk of rock has an integral quality of "firmness" that is more so than a scrap of satin. Sometimes they are more subtle, and not easy to see right off without much experimentation, which is where we get all those lists of what rock or plant or color has what magical properties. You'll see some of those lists in this book. They were created through someone else's trial and error, which means that they're only as accurate as we fallible humans can make them.

You have to work a balance between what your lizard brain wants and the innate vibrations of physical objects. If you read that the best stone for grounding is hematite, and you can't stand the stuff, find another stone with similar properties that you can stand, or your lizard brain will probably sabotage the whole process out of pique. You can't fight your lizard brain and win—where magic is concerned, anyway. You have to negotiate and coax, or you get nowhere.

Some people may need to lean to one side or the other. One end of the spectrum leans to the kind of thing that we gently mocked in the third paragraph of this chapter—the mage with his lists and lists of picayune details, and everything set up just so. The advantage to this is that it's very formulaic; you know you'll get more or less the same thing every time, and it works when your lizard brain is confused or doesn't know what it wants. It can be very good for people who have trouble with even the basics of sensing energy—the ones who miss again and again on the simple energy exercise detailed above. Doing things via the ceremonial route, over and over again, will eventually burn the track into your head, and your senses will line up with the energy.

On the other side are people who do the whole thing instinctively, leaning toward the shamanic rather than the ceremonial. The classic idea of these folks is the old wisewoman or cunning man who wanders about the woods picking things up—"This feels like strength, and this feels like vengeance, and this looks like power"—and ties them together, chants something unintelligible, waves a cigarette, and it's done. Some people prefer to work this way, letting their lizard brain call all the shots. Some people find that they start out more structured and slowly evolve into a more instinctive mode over time.

your magical tool kit

Some physical items, however, you're going to want to keep around to work with on frequent occasions. These will be your magical tools, and they can be anything, anything at all. They don't have to be the basic kit of one knife, one cup, one censer, and so on. (Although again, if that turns you on, that's fine.) They will need to be charged, and cleansed and recharged, on occasion. They will need to be treated with respect. That's the only bottom line.

We'll give you two examples of the tools we use the most, just to show you how diverse any two magicians' preferences can be.

TANNIN'S BASIC TOOL KIT

1 hunting knife

1 staff—a 5½-foot former flagpole

Mortar and pestle

Variety of colored candles and candleholders

1 broom

1 Tarot deck

1 dozen or so empty jars of various shapes and sizes

1 bunch of fake flowers

Box of random bones, beads, rocks, and metal bits

2 strands of small bells

Collection of incenses and oils that would knock your socks off

RAVEN'S BASIC TOOL KIT

1 agricultural sickle bought at a yard sale

1 fan made of chicken feathers

1 pocket lockblade knife

1 hourglass-shaped egg timer

Bunch of keys

1 lighter

Random candle stubs

1 cup usually grabbed out of the kitchen cabinet

Many ribbon and fabric scraps

1 large chunk of hematite

A superb selection of bits of dried herb and other plant matter

1 drum

1 guitar

We are not suggesting that you collect these as your tools; these are simply examples of what we've come down to using most often over the years. Your tool kit may have some of these things, or none of them; it will be as individual as you are. The only thing the tools will all have in common is that you will have filled them with energy, both through deliberate charging and regular usage.

popular building blocks

Candles are a popular building block for spells in many traditions. First you should decide what purpose the candle spell will have. Usually the color of the candle is chosen for this purpose, using either a list of traditional "purpose" colors (below) or whatever color your lizard brain suggests. Another easy and useful traditional building block are oils, which come in an astounding array of herb, flower, animal, and mineral flavors. Oils are used both as a vehicle for the caster's energy and, depending on what's in them, to add a little extra pep to the spell.

We realize that oils are often prohibitively expensive, and we are including a list to show you how to substitute cheaper substances for traditional (and costly) oils. In a pinch, you can charge a tool or candle with the oils on your own skin. Run your fingers over the greasiest part of your body, be it your hair, face, or whatever, and rub it on the item while producing energy. It will act as a carrier. (This is also a good way to magically mark territory.)

Oils may be either essential or diluted. Essential oils are very strong and you may not want to apply them directly to your skin; ones like peppermint or cinnamon can burn, and pennyroyal oil can be poisonous. Dilute it with a neutral oil such as almond, grapeseed, canola, or even corn. Heavier vegetable oils may not blend perfectly, so be sure to shake them up before using them.

Charging tools or candles is easy. The shape is irrelevant. Find whatever you would call the middle of the thing, generate your energy using whatever technique you want, focus on the result of your goal (for example, if it's a prosperity spell, imagine the money in your hand), and rub in the oil from the center outward. This is to push out whatever's in it, and put in what you want. The more time and energy you put into it, the stronger it'll be, but we'd suggest at least five minutes at a minimum. You can reuse used candles if you cleanse them (see chapter 4, Internal Hygiene).

With novena-style candles (that's the ones in the big jars) some will be pull-outs, meaning you can pull the candle out, oil it (and stick things to it) and put it back, and some will be stuck there, and you'll have to oil the top while forcing power through the bottom with your hand.

You can charge a candle in little bits of time over several days, as long as it's a continuous and regular process. It's hard to keep energy in an item that isn't being used, so don't let something lie for weeks without touching it and then expect it to work without recharging. Charged candles can be kept wrapped in butcher paper or wax paper. In general, charged magical supplies should be stored somewhere they will not be disturbed, and not shown to others. For magical tools, it's your call.

oil substitution chart

Many essential oils are rare and made from special imported ingredients. This may make them too expensive and hard to find for the average low-budget magical practitioner. Fortunately there are more common oils that can be substituted that have similar properties. For many of the oils that are animal products, what is sold in stores isn't really the actual oil, but a synthesized version. The store owner may not even know which are which. Sometimes it's better to use a substitution oil that's natural than a synthetic one that smells like the real thing.

Amber. Made from fossilized tree sap from ancient coniferous trees. Substitute piñon pine tree resin with a little frankincense mixed in. It's not as sweet, but it will do.

Ambergris. Real ambergris is a digestive enzyme found in whale vomit, gathered either from whale slaughter or scooping the stuff off the water. Its natural form is a resin, but many stores have banned it because of whaling practices, and it's hard to get it. Much of what is sold as ambergris is synthetic. Substitute honey if you're using it for a love spell, or even real maple syrup (not artificially flavored pancake syrup). If it's for a protection spell, use any strong floral scent, such as jasmine, rose, or gardenia.

Asafoetida. The ultimate smelly banishing plant; you can sometimes find it in ground form in Indian groceries, but the oil is hard to come by. Substitute garlic oil.

Attar of Roses. Real Attar of Roses is the extracted oil of one particular variety of rose, the Turkish Kazanlik Damask rose. Most Attar of Roses is simply rose oil, and most rose oil is actually artificial. Some of it is actually rose geranium oil; some is synthesized scent. You can get actual roses from the florist (or the dumpster behind the florist's shop) and rub them on the candle.

Civet. Actual civet comes from the musk glands of the civet cat, which is endangered. Most civet oil is fake. Use the same replacements as musk (see below).

Cypress. Oil of the cypress tree, native to Greece and a rare import. For a spell, substitute cedar oil. If it is an offering to the Death Goddess (its ritual use), you'd better use the real thing or find something entirely different that she'll accept, such as a drop of your own blood.

Dragon's Blood. Real dragon's blood is the resin from the dragon's blood tree, which only grows in certain tropical countries. Whenever there is a blight, the price skyrockets. Most things labeled dragon's blood oil are not. The real stuff has an earthy, pungent smell, not a sweet or spicy one like the faux stuff. Substitute tobacco in a protection spell, preferably from a good cigar, mixed with some oil. For love spells or power-boosting spells, use cinnamon oil. (Don't put either of these on your skin.)

Frankincense. Solar oil. Substitute bay oil, or something citrusy like lemon or orange, or even plain old sunflower oil.

Mandrake. Really hard to find, in root or oil form. For protective spells, substitute tobacco. For power boosting, use pennyroyal oil. For love spells, use strong floral scents.

Musk. Real musk comes from the scent glands of the musk ox. Most of the musk oil sold in stores is artificial, and has a sickly, sweetish smell. Substitute vetivert oil, which is more common as it's used worldwide as an erosion-control plant, or else patchouli.

Myrrh. Some people say feminine solar, some say lunar. If you see it as feminine solar, substitute a combination of vetivert and lemon, in a ratio of about 3 to 1. If you are working with it as a lunar scent, substitute eucalyptus oil. You can even substitute Vicks in a pinch, although you should not burn it, as it is petroleum based.

Neroli. Real neroli is from the blossom of a particular species of orange. It's usually real, but terribly expensive. Heat sliced orange peel in water and use that, or soak the peel in oil.

Note: If you use perfume instead of essential oil, be very careful and don't apply it to a candle. Perfumes have a lot of alcohol content and can catch fire easily, especially when sprayed near a candle flame. Don't cause explosions as part of your spells.

tannin and raven's captain chaos variable color chart

Use to design spells for candles, cords, bits of paper, and so on.

Red. Color of Mars. Associated with the element of Fire. Red is the most passionate color, and that means all passions—anger, lust, hate, enthusiasm, love, obsession, and so on. Red is aggression, warrior stuff, blood and childbirth, anything that involves both desire and struggle. Your lizard brain should decide whether or not red suggests the more positive or more negative of these passions to you.

Dark red. This is separate from scarlet as it is specifically the color of blood, and of blood rites. Blood rites can be anything from menstruation to childbirth to sacrifice. Dark red is a deep and powerful color, and should be used with caution, or at least only if you know what you're doing.

Orange. Made notorious by the 1970s. Orange is one of the solar colors, and denotes courage and strong energy. It's the energy-boost color, and on the downside it can give out so much energy that it can be irritating and hyperactive.

(A quote from a friend of ours: "I'm an urban Autumn! My colors are hospital green, safety orange, and police-line yellow!")

Yellow. Color of the sun and the life force. In China, it's happiness; in certain parts of Africa, it's associated with love because it's the color of honey. In the West it's been associated with everything from cowardice to plague to prostitution, as well as intellectualism! It can be used to draw aid or a mentor, or to make things "sunnier." One of its more dastardly uses, specifically for bright screaming yellow, is to instill panic. Gold, its softer cousin, generally has all the positive and none of the negative connotations of yellow; it has its own negative connotation, greed, as a sideline to its most popular use, prosperity magic.

Green. When the authors of the book *Dress for Success* did research into what clothing colors made the best impression in the corporate world, green was the absolute bottom of the list. This is extremely ironic, considering that green is the color of prosperity and abundance. However, it implies a certain laissez-faire abundance that is hedonistic and in tune with Nature, which apparently is anathema to the corporate workplace. Green is love that is compassionate, possibly platonic, and often parental. It is a color of healing and regeneration; however, your more earthy greens, along with brown, can be used to conceal things, as in camouflage. Chartreuse and other yellow-greens are symbolic of disease. Green is also the hunting color, and is said to be the color of the fairies. It is the color of the Earth and fertility, and all its varied meanings are tied together by being basically Earth- or body-linked.

Blue. This is the most soothing of all colors, but it can vary greatly, depending on shade. It is universally acclaimed to be the color of the element Water, but like water, it can be mild and tranquil (light blue) or sorrowful (dark blue). In the Middle Ages, blue was the color of servants, and today in America it is the color of denim and the working class. It has also taken on the connotation of dealing with the law (the blue people!), and generally connotes clearheadedness and mercy.

Purple. In ancient times, purple was royalty, the VIP color. You can use purple in order to impress people above your class, like a VIP mask spell. It is also used as a psychic protection color, and increases self-esteem. Lavender, its pastel version, has a specifically feminine bent to it, with connotations in this culture ranging from grandmothers to lesbians.

Pink. Color of Venus, although some assign that to green. Love, babies, cuddles, affection.

Brown. Color of the Earth. It's been used both to curse and to remove curses. What it seems to be most associated with, in the human mind, is feces, so it can be cleansing and absorbing of negativity (psychic feces). Some (less ethical) folk will use this color to fling their "energy dung" on someone else. It's also good for motivational magic that has to do with work: When you need to slog through the unappealing task that must be done, use brown. It's the color of work—not career or money, but the daily grind. It's an earthy, physical color that is close to Nature.

Grey. The color of depression, confusion, and, strangely enough, neutrality. It's good for binding spells, camouflage, and obscuring something. Grey can neutralize a strong, passionate spell or situation, or hide things. It is also the color of sleep. The darker the grey, the more depressing it is. Silver, a metallic version of grey, is the color of the moon, and somewhat different. Although moon energy does obscure and make things different, silver is associated with imagination, intuition, and dreams.

White. The color of purity and cleanliness. White can be pretty harsh sometimes. Although being scrubbed clean can be great, it can also make you raw. White can be used to expose truth, but it's usually a brutal truth. White is the color of the maiden and thus of innocence but, as everyone knows, innocent children are the first to blurt out painful and embarrassing things. White can be great in goodness and great in self-righteousness. Too much white light casts a very dark shadow. The element of Air has been associated with white, but in some traditions it's yellow, and in others light blue. In the East, white is the color of death and mourning because the corpse is pale.

Black. The color of power. That's why it's worn by priests, judges, high-ranking executives, and Death. Black suggests night, where things are hidden. There is a certain fatality to black; it's about necessity, severity, and that which cannot be turned aside. Black is "blacklisted" in a lot of old fuddy-duddy magical books that will tell you not to use it at all, as it has been associated with death, destruction, and harm. Other old fuddy-duddy witches will tell you that all witches should wear black because it will absorb and deflect negativity. We leave it up to you. Remember that black has the biggest magical "kick" of all colors; it lends authority and oomph to your energy.

Knot Magic

Another quick-and dirty simple spell is knot magic. Get a piece of yarn, string, or thread—we prefer embroidery thread, but you can use ordinary thin thread if you want extra camouflage. Wave it through burning incense, or just hold it and charge it mentally in your hands. Then tie knots in it, a minimum of three. One useful thing to say as you tie a three-knot spell is, "I send out my will, I beseech the cosmos, I accept the return." Another old traditional knot spell using nine knots goes like this:

By knot of one, the spell's begun,

By knot of two, I make it true,

By knot of three, so mote it be,

By knot of four, the open door,

By knot of five, the spell's alive,

(This is your last chance to stop. After this, the spell has gone too far to turn back.)

By knot of six, the spell is fixed,

By knot of seven, the earth and heaven,

By knot of eight, the stroke of fate,

By knot of nine, the thing is mine.

Magical knots can be stitched into anything made of fabric; they provide an easy way to make a portable and unobtrusive spell. A good way to do it is to take out a small edge of the lining of a lined garment such as a coat, stitch the knot to the inside, and then restitch the lining closed. Obviously, if you know how to knit or crochet, you can do really big knot magic works; just focus the energy periodically while working on a specific piece.

Bag Magic

Probably the oldest and most eclectic type of spell is bag magic. You just get a little bag—and a piece of cloth with a string to tie it up with will do as well—and put in it a bunch of things that seem all-of-a-theme to you. Anything goes: rocks, plant matter, colored wax bits, tiny knickknacks, stuff out of gum machines, pennies, salt or pepper or sugar in little packets from the fast-food restaurant. (Salt is for grounding, pepper for energy, and sugar for love and happiness. Got it?) All that is required is that the theme hangs together in your mind. Then just seal it up, knot the string (a knot spell works good here), and either carry it on your person or hang it from the mirror in your car or whatever.

Portable Altars

City people move a lot. We are often on the go, and do a lot of fast travel in our cars or on the subway or bus. Your big, elaborate altar isn't very useful when you need to make a quick trip to a friend's house using two buses and a subway car, and will have to set up a spell as soon as you get there. Putting together a portable altar for emergency or travel use is your best bet.

You'll want to start with some kind of box with a handle, like a small suitcase or briefcase. The best version we've ever seen was a former portable bar someone had trashpicked, with all the little straps for holding items of various sizes in place. If you don't have such straps, we recommend you put them in so that things don't rattle around. You can cut the buckle and hole ends off of old, worn belts and staple, rivet, or glue them in place. Some suggestions for filling the box are as follows:

Chalice. Use a shot glass, tiny plastic wineglass, eggcup, or other small cup. Some religious supply places have small three- or four-inch plastic or metal goblets. Include a small plastic soda bottle of water, tightly capped, with a couple of appropriate stones in it to energize it. You can't guarantee you'll always be in a place with a faucet.

Wand, small. A carved stick or piece of copper tubing with a stone in one end works.

Small, framed pictures of deities. These can be magazine cutouts. Raven's wife framed a tiny picture of Zippy the Pinhead as the Sacred Fool, and a pair of lovers for Aphrodite.

Any herbs, spices, or powdered or cone incense you need, in unbreakable containers. Plastic film canisters work great.

Film canister of shiny, polished coins for money spells. Also works well for emergency phone money or bus fare.

Small mirror. For doing self-improvement spells. A compact works fine. You can pull the makeup out of the other side and put in a picture or photo.

Little plastic figurines, glued or tied in. Toy soldiers for warrior spirit, little dolls dressed appropriately for the gods, plastic animals for totem figures.

Athame. This can be a small penknife, nail file, or letter opener.

Votive candle in metal—not glass—holder, with matches in plastic bag. Lighters leak and are less safe, although they will work if you really prefer it.

Old key, steel. For symbolizing wisdom and drawing lines on pavement or brick.

Piece of sidewalk chalk. Use it to make non-permanent markings (bind runes, sigils, protective circles, etc.) on floors, streets, and sidewalks. If you visualize burning the magick in as you make the mark, it will remain after the chalk has been washed away.

Writing utensils. Pencil (pens dry up or leak) with small, school-type sharpener and pad of two-inch, stick-on notepaper.

Nail polish. Tightly capped bottle in a bright color. Use for marking runes or symbols on things.

Chewing gum. A pack that you can stand to taste. Use for sticking things to other things. Since it will have your bodily fluids on it, it will be that much more powerful.

The idea is that everything should be lightweight, portable, unbreakable, easily replaced if lost or stolen, and easily misinterpreted by passersby who might happen to see it.

three

Defenses

PROTECTION INSIDE AND OUT

"I believe that the city dweller needs, even more than the country dweller, to define a boundary between My Space and The Outside World. I have wards at all my doorways, and a permanent ritual circle embedded in the walls of my house, not because I feel the need for protection, but because I feel more comfortable with a barrier between 'me' and 'the rest of the world.' The outside world does not impinge much on my personal space, and when it does it has a reason."

BETH HARPER, NASHVILLE WITCH

• • The very first magic that you need to learn in the city is protective magic; this is basic, elementary stuff. You will need to protect yourself against two kinds of trouble: physical attack and psychic grind. Physical attack is pretty straightforward, from muggers to purse-snatchers, but you will also need protection against the general psychic dirt and grime of the city itself, which as a magic-worker you will be more open to.

These two areas break down further into personal and home protection; stuff you carry on your body, and stuff you do to your homespace. We'll start with the first part.

Personal Protection

When you walk out the door every day, you want to feel safe walking down the street. You'll want to be protected from assault, both verbal and physical, and accidents. Make sure to work any personal protection spells on a bright, sunny day in full light. This not only adds strong solar energy, but also imbues the charm with the best protection of all: being able to see well enough to get out of the way.

The easiest method of protection spell is to wear something on the body. Charms that are carried on the torso and head are more efficacious than ones on the arms or legs. Wearing a charm on the head is particularly good if you are expecting an attack and want to see it coming. General physical protection spells should be worn on the torso. The usual one is a mojo bag made of several items either wrapped in cloth and tied with a string, or in a small cloth bag. Suggested items might be salt, pepper, gingerroot (or, if you can find and afford it, High John the Conqueror root), the tooth of a large or predatory animal, or a small toy weapon such as a sword or gun. Wear it on your person, under your clothes, or on a hat.

Stones are strongly protective. Traditional semiprecious stones that confer protection are hematite (for bodily well-being), lapis lazuli (for defense against hexes), and staurolite or fairy crosses (for powerful general-purpose protection). Turquoise protects specifically for travel on anything that moves—horses, cars, trains, planes, and so on. In the old days, turquoise rings were worn by people who were constantly on horseback, and were sometimes worked into horse tack. Labradorite, also called spectrolite, was used for protection in traveling over water, such as shipboard travel. However, if you can't afford fancy rocks, any small, round stone can be considered "elf-shot" if its energy seems right—elf-shot being the tiny arrowheads believed by medieval people to be the "shot" of the faeries, which could harm or protect a human. Also, any stone with a natural hole in it is automatically strongly magical; a "holey" stone is a good thing to have. Go looking for rocks and pebbles that feel right. If you're not sure, close your eyes and grab in a pebbly or gravelly area. The right one will find its way into your hand. Add it to your mojo bag.

For those people who have holes poked in their bodies, protection spells can be semipermanently affixed to existing piercings or can be piercings in and of themselves. Piercing rings often have stone beads, which have magical vibrations. Hematite is useful for protection against physical attack, while lapis lazuli or bloodstone defends against psychic attack. There are actual piercing rings and plugs made of polished stone as well, and it is fairly nonreactive and safe, more so than most metals, at least. (See chapter 11, Tribal Markings, in which we discuss safety and what you should and shouldn't put through your flesh.) You can hang small wooden charms with runes off of a piercing, or little saint's medals, if you're into that sort of thing. Of course, the biggest, best, and most permanent protection spell is a tattoo. These are infamous—many people with multiple tattoos have ones specifically as protective devices.

If you want a less permanent and more short-term protection spell, such as for a trip through a difficult area of town, a temporary tattoo (easy and cheap) can be placed on any area of your body. It need not be visible, and it can lie safely under your clothing; but you can also, if you choose, locate it somewhere strategic for maximum effect. As an example, a woman we know who had very large and beautiful breasts was often harassed on the street by passersby, except when wearing the bulkiest of coats. When construction workers did a job outside her place of work, mornings became a regular gauntlet of verbal abuse for her. Knowing that they would be there for at least a week, she found two temporary tattoos of the ugliest gargoyles she could find and stuck one to each breast, under her clothing. From then on, the men suddenly stopped harassing her, and indeed looked vaguely disturbed when she came by, and found other things to look at. Temporary tattoos last two to three days; if you want a longer spell, you'd best stock up. However, we suggest that if you need to replace an old, peeling tattoo, that you do not situate the new one directly on top of where the old one was. Put it a few inches away for the sake of possible skin irritations.

Home Protection

When it comes to your home, what you'll ideally want to do is to create a web of energy that extends all around it and filters out everything from the outside. Your homespace should be a haven of peace and psychic silence; if you're doing regular magic work and checking in with the spirit of the city, or helping others with their problems, or just going out daily to survive, you need that silent homespace in which to recuperate. The extra energy you put into cleansing and shielding your home will pay off in the end.

Many of us aren't rich, and don't own or rent entire buildings in the city. In fact, if you live in a large city, the most likely living arrangement for you to have is to be renting a small room or series of rooms in a large human-anthill apartment complex. Doing protective magic to shield your tiny space from the angry vibes of neighbors arguing on the other side of thin walls is not easy, but it's not impossible either.

The best space-protective magic is layers of spells, each one interlocking into the next. This sounds difficult, but it's not; you just "select from the menu" a handful of protection spells that work for you and your space, and do them one at a time, spaced about a day apart. See each one as another layer of soft but strong shielding, wrapping your space up like a baby in blankets. The different layers will protect against different things, like various filters.

Start with the outside of your building. Even if it's a big apartment complex full of other people's rooms, the first layer should enclose the entire building. After all, you'll want to feel safe on the steps and in the hall as well as in your own rooms. You can do this with plain old salt, or salt and herbs, or salt and spices. If you add herbs to the mix, you can either get traditional "rural" protective herbs, assuming you have a source, or use city plants that you might find around. Examples of traditional protective herbs include bay, agrimony, rue, sage, and pennyroyal. City plants that have protective vibrations include knotgrass, mullein, plantain, and oak leaves. You can chop or powder them, or keep the leaves whole. Appropriate spices include white and black pepper, cayenne, or crumbled chili peppers. Another really good thing to use is cornmeal; in a pinch, even granola or crumbled cold cereal will work. Mix the whole mess together with the salt and walk around the building clockwise, sprinkling so that it falls along the edge of the foundation. While you're doing this activity, picture protective energy growing up out of the ground and surrounding the building like ivy or vines crawling over the whole place, growing in fast motion.

Next, protect the building's doors. Make sure that the line of the salt mix crosses just outside the threshold of each door, and put an extra amount there. If there is an actual patch of earth by the door, such as a bed for flowers or foundation plantings, bury a small bottle there. Use a soda bottle and fill it with stones, nails, tacks, pins, small plastic guns (you can cut them off of small plastic soldiers), and other sharp or dangerous-looking items. Add salt. Cork it and bury it facing away from the steps.

If there is no earth next to your door but only cement or asphalt, paint protective symbols on it with some clear but substantial liquid such as vegetable oil. It doesn't have to last or show; in fact, it may be better if it doesn't. Nosy neighbors need not know what you're doing, and the effects will remain on the astral level.

Another good door protection spell is to mix up some oil and soot and paint protective symbols on the risers of each step. Most people don't notice stair risers; their perspective is that of looking down at the top of the step. Any stairs with no risers at all, where you can get to the underneath part of the step, are especially good. You can paint protective symbols on the undersides and it's likely no one will see them. For metal fire-escape-type stairs with perforations in the treads, you can hang small items so that they dangle just under the tread. Don't use thread; wire them on with paper clips or Christmas ornament hangers, and place them to one side where the wires are less likely to be noticed or catch someone's shoe.

Now pay attention to the doors to your own apartment or, if you live in a group house, your own room. Repeat the sprinkling of the salt-and-stuff mix across your threshold, and draw a protective rune on the door with your finger dipped in the oil-and-soot mix. If you use Norse runes, Othila is good (ᛟ). Then, on the inside, you can hang things on your door. Bells are good, as are horseshoes and small weapons, such as toy guns or sword pendants.

One of the most impressive door-protection spells you can do is this: Go down to the butcher and ask for chicken feet. Some of the butchers or grocers that cater to ethnic groups will have them. Buy or make a small toy gun or sword. Wrap the chicken foot's toes around the weapon as if it is holding it—if it's a gun, put one claw through the trigger—and wrap it in place with lots of string. Then put the whole thing in a pan and cover it entirely with salt (any kind, though we prefer kosher or sea salt). Leave it for a month in a warm, dry place, after which time it will be completely preserved and mummified, and should hold its shape when you take the string off. If it doesn't hold the weapon perfectly of its own accord, it's okay to use some glue. Then hang it, pointing down, over your most-used door, and picture it only harming those who enter to do you and yours harm.

Then it's time to deal with the rest of the living space. Start with a basic space purification ritual (see Internal Hygiene, chapter 4) and make sure that you get every room. Trace your finger, dipped in the oil, along the baseboards of every wall that has the outside world or someone else's space on the other side. As you do it, visualize a bubble of shielding growing around your space, transparent as a soap bubble but harder than steel, a force field. Hang something in each window—a god's-eye made from yarn and sticks, glass bottles with food-coloring water in them, and so on. If you can make something that resembles an eye, so much the better. Hang them facing outward in windows that look out onto the main approach to the building. Your house now has eyes and will warn you when trouble is coming.

Mirrors strategically placed in windows are a good way to keep away negative or erratic energy floating about. They are specifically better for psychic protection than physical attack, and they will deflect outside chaos and pain. Mirrors are a standard item in the Feng Shui arsenal (see Feng Shui section in the Migration chapter) and are used to increase the spiritual area of part of a house that is too small, or to reflect "bad spirits" away from an "unlucky" doorway or turn of hall.

Bedrooms and beds need special protection, because those are where you will lie at your most vulnerable. Even if no one is actually attempting to harm you magically, the energy from outside can sometimes drift in through all the layers and filter into your dreams—especially if the people on the other side of the wall are fighting or otherwise having a bad time.

Traditional charms to hang at the head of the bed, tuck under the pillow, or stick between the mattresses are small mojo bags of dill, lemon verbena, chamomile, or eucalyptus, singly or in combination. If you don't have access to herbs, wrap a handful of cotton balls in a cloth and tie it up with white thread, so that you may sleep as if buoyed on soothing, fluffy clouds. Children especially like this. For anti-nightmare spells, see chapter 12, Offspring, where we have put together an entire arsenal.

psychic home cleansing

Remember that your house needs to be cleansed psychically at least once a year, and ideally at each turning of the seasons. You need protection not only from external energies, but from your own grouchiness as well, and that of your family. The problem with layers of protection spells is that they often have the same effect that overinsulating a house might: It's warm and cozy, and no cold gets in, but you're all breathing each others' air and there's little or no ventilation. Inside this sealed nest, the psychic vibes can build up over time. Since "emotion" is "energy in motion," and it has to have a place to go, people's personal bad vibes can collect to the point where the place feels psychically stuffy. When your kids are eager to get outside each morning, and friends don't stop by for very long, and you find yourself becoming irritable over little things, house/space purification is in order. (See chapter 4, Internal Hygiene.) Of course, it might just be that the cat's litter box needs cleaning. Be sure to check.

In the jungle of the city, your home is your fortress, and it will be worth your while to make it a safe-feeling place, even if it's only temporary digs. The price you'll pay in alleviating paranoia and raw nerves alone is worth it. Remember that if you bother to put the right kind of attention into the magic, it'll work, and there will be one place in the world where no one can harm you, unless you let them in. But that's another mistake for another chapter.

four

Internal Hygiene

HOW TO NOT GET UGLY

• • You're logy and irritable and easily tired out. You start at unfamiliar noises. You keep washing, but never quite feel clean for more than a few minutes. You feel as if something's pressing down on you all the time. You're hard to be around.

Sound familiar? Well, you could just be suffering from depression, or vitamin deficiency, or something else physical. If you're an urban dweller, there is, however, the possibility that the city's energy is just getting to you, that you're stained and soiled and need a good psychic laundering.

The best of all possible worlds is a good, long visit away from the place, but we may not have the wherewithal to do this. Not all of us can afford Caribbean vacations or even country visits. There are jobs to get to and money that can't be spent. You need to do something now, tonight, or you're going to scream.

Purification Spells

There are two basic kinds of purification spells, just as there are two basic defense spells: personal and place-oriented. We'll start with personal.

Personal purification is generally done for two reasons. The first, and simplest, is simply to clean off the psychic gook that you may have collected in your channels throughout the day. This is exceptionally important if you live in an urban environment. The second kind is purification that you do in preparation for some large magical working or ritual.

One of the most common forms of purification is done with smoke, using some kind of smoking or smudging. You can use the smoke from any number of herbs, resins, or woods and bathe yourself in smoke from head to toe. This is best done nude, but can be done with clothing on, if necessary. Drop the plant matter onto a charcoal disk in a heatproof vessel and light the disk. Mind you, some herbs are better for some sorts of purification than others.

suggested herbs for smudging

Agrimony, rue, and vervain. This is for when you are going up against ghosts, spirits, or other heavies. Smells pretty bad, but has the cleansing effect of a psychic grenade.

Asafoetida. THIS STINKS! Use for emergencies only, when you're in serious trouble, lost in a morass of evil. You won't like it. Neither will your pets, friends, and housemates (whom you'd better talk to before you so fumigate the house), but it does do the trick.

Cedar. One of the original funereal woods, cedar was used to invoke such things as precognition. It gets your psychic channels, such as your third eye, clear for divinatory work.

Dragon's blood. Love it or hate it. Very pungent, weird smell. Earthy and spicy. Potent purifier, very masculine energy. Associated with dragons and, therefore, ancient wisdom. (**Note:** Real dragon's blood is a resin. When bought in large quantities, it comes in a dense, rock-like mass that is brick-red to brown. When cut, it is somewhat sticky to the touch. Don't be fooled by bright powders that claim to be dragon's blood.)

Frankincense. Big in Egyptian magic, frankincense has solar energy used to clean and cleanse with the power of the sun. Sweet-smelling and benedictive.

Myrrh. Also used in Egyptian magic. Some traditions say it's solar, some traditions say it's lunar. Has a more feminine energy than frankincense, with darker and headier musk. Often combined with frankincense.

Sage, rosemary, and thyme. Like the song. These common European garden herbs can be used straight out of your spice cabinet or purchased in the spice section of the store. They have a sweet, homey smell and are simple benediction herbs. They can be bought pre-ground and powdered; if you buy them in stem-and-leaf form, we suggest grinding them as finely as you can before burning. The finer the powder, the better it works with charcoal.

Sandalwood. Sacred to various love goddesses. Really pleasant smell. Gives a cleansing tinged with happiness and sensuality. Good for days when you don't like your body.

Sweetgrass. Used to call spirits to you—any and all spirits. This is a tradition, again, of the native Southwestern folk, and was used after the cedar and sagebrush combination to call ancestors and various deities.

Tarragon. Used for courage, as *tarragon* means "little dragon." It's a strong smell and will give you guts when you need them.

White sagebrush. The most common, a gentle purifier from the indigenous peoples of the American Southwest, not the common sage in your kitchen. This is good for soothing and calming, but not much good for serious banishing. Often accompanied by cedar.

the not recommended list

You may find recipes for cleansing incenses with these herbs. We don't suggest that you use them, for safety reasons, as they are lung irritants.

Bloodroot. A mucous membrane irritant. Don't use.

Orris root. Used as a base in many old recipes. Irritates.

Pepper. Black, white, or cayenne. Burns clear and fine, and puts a haze throughout the air that will cause long-lasting coughing and a river of mucus. Hangs around for a while, too.

Other. Poisonous herbs such as henbane, hemlock, belladonna, datura, bittersweet, foxglove, oleander, and buttercup. Don't be stupid.

Purification with Baths

The problem with smudging is that it always involves smoke. People with asthma or sensitive fire alarms may want to use a different method. The next most common purification method is baths. You will need a bathtub for most of them, although we will include shower formulas for those of you with only shower stalls.

floral bath

Soothing, calming, and brightening for depressed days. Also good for getting one in a romantic mood, not just before a date but when the magic is going out of a long-term relationship due to stress and exhaustion. You can either use floral oils such as jasmine, rose, lavender, or apple blossom, or live flower petals. For the destitute, check dumpsters behind florist shops and pull the petals off the discarded, bruised flowers. You will need at least two cups of flower petals. If you're worried about clogging the drain, put them in a bag (even an old T-shirt with the holes knotted shut will do) and float them in the water. If you like them floating around on the water, put a piece of fabric over the drain when you let the water out.

herbal baths

Cook the herbs into a strong tea on the stove and pour them into the water. Simmer, do not boil. Suggested herbs include sage, rosemary, thyme (see above), tarragon for courage, ground sandalwood for sensuality, bay leaf for warrior energy, or mint and eucalyptus to promote physical health. Resins will not break down when boiled. If you want to use a resin, you must add the essential oil or absolute (resin tincture).

shower formulas

For this, you need to brew up one to three gallons of strong tea. Take your shower first, like you normally do, and then at whatever temperature you can tolerate, dump the pots of water over your body. These teas can be boiled and set aside in gallon plastic jugs for when you want them—in the hot summer, you may want to dump them over you cold. Don't keep them for more than a week, and check them frequently for nasty, green floating things or bad smells.

steam baths

Yes, this can be done in an apartment, if you have big pots and a stove. Fill all your large pots with boiling water and add herbs or oils. Fill the tub half full with the hottest water you can get from the tap, and place a chair in the tub. (If you use a metal chair, rest your hand on it before sitting down to test the temperature. If it is wooden, make sure you have a place for it to dry out afterwards. Avoid padded chairs as they will absorb moisture and get mildewy.) Then pour in the boiling water and sit on the chair, being careful not to touch the water. Relax in the steam until the water cools.

the white bath

Famous in Afro-Caribbean traditions. It is associated with the Orisha (deity) Obatala, who represents justice, compassion, and healing. The most common ingredient in a white bath is coconut milk, usually canned, since if you use real coconuts, you'll have to split a lot of them. Other suggestions are baking soda, or sugar, or a few drops of vanilla extract, or powdered milk. Powdered moo-juice will last forever and may be carried with you anywhere. You can combine any or all of these, but no more than two cups of material per tubful. For dissolving purposes, make sure the water is pretty hot. Soak for as long as you need, and then rinse off with the shower. Lighting white candles around the tub is also good, as is coconut incense.

Although you will want to rinse off at some point, we recommend that you wait at least twenty minutes before rinsing, in order to let the energy of each bath soak into your skin as you get up and move about. It's traditional, though not necessary, to wear only white for the first few hours afterwards. (A really big T-shirt works well.) If you hate white, you don't have to wear it, but please, whatever you put on should be clean and freshly laundered, and also have clean towels ready to dry off with.

Purification with Sound

Another cleansing method is using sound. Here, you'll have to be careful not to wake your neighbors, especially if you live somewhere with thin walls. A fairly quiet method is to use either bells or tuning forks, and jingle or tap them all around your body, in turn bathing each part of your aura in the sound. The noisy method requires a good stereo with decent speakers, and neighbors who won't kill you. Put headphones on your ears, put your speakers so they face each other about two feet apart, put on music, and stand between them. Don't funnel the music through the headphones; they are ear protection. The music should be coming out the speakers, and be really, really loud. What we've found works best is stuff that isn't too fast or raucous, has a strong, deep, booming bass line, and doesn't have too much high, screaming parts.

Basic Space Purification Ritual

Sometimes the mental debris of many people's problems piles up until the space itself needs a good cleansing. You can do purification spells on your home, place of work, the inside of your car (how many of us have arguments while driving!), or anywhere else that you can get in and do what you need to do without being thrown out. You can do it different ways, as well, depending on the type of space—there's full-blown ritual, or discreet, invisible ritual. You can do the first kind in your own home, but you might want to resort to the second kind at work or in a public area.

For a full-blown space purification ritual, you'll need the following:

Large candle, preferably in a jar

Large cup of water

Smudge or incense of some kind

Small branch of a tree or green plant, even a weed

A compass, to tell the directions

A broom

Things to bang on—can be drums, tambourines, plastic jugs, pots and pans, glass jars to ding, whatever you can come up with

This ritual can be done by only one person, although it will take longer and you'll have to carry everything from room to room. However, it is best done with all the denizens of the house taking part, as they've all taken part in creating the mess. If they all refuse to help and you are left to do it yourself, it will still work fine even without their input, but it's stronger with all hands on deck, as it were. Since it's noisy, you may want to warn neighbors if you live in an apartment building. Assure them that it won't take very long.

Start at the bottom of the house. If it's an apartment, start at the front door or even the downstairs hallway. If it's a house with a basement, start there. We recommend the compass because not everyone knows where east is in the depths of their basement. Call out, "I purify this place in the name of the spirits of the east!" and wave the smudge or incense stick in every corner. Then call out, "I purify this place in the name of the spirits of the south!" and wave the lit candle in each corner. Repeat for the spirits of the west, sprinkling a few drops of water in each corner (make sure you filled the cup enough to do every corner of every room in the house), and then repeat for the spirits of the north, waving the green twig at each corner.

While this is going on, ideally your helpers should be chanting and banging and making as much noise as they possibly can. Different people can be assigned to each element, or one person can do all the elements while the others simply make noise. Try to find a good, easy rhythm, possibly even nonverbal, like *YA-da-da-da, YA-da-da-da*—something that everyone can follow along with even while mounting stairs and/or giggling. One person should go ahead of all the others as they move from room to room, sweeping the air with the broom ahead of them.

The procession should progress from the bottom of the house to the very top. Hallways and bathrooms count as rooms, as do stairwells if they're big enough. Closets should be opened and waved at, especially if they're walk-ins. At the top of the house, or the end of the apartment, in the final room, open a window (yes, even if it's really cold out, it doesn't have to be for long) and sweep the last of the bad energy out with great dramatic motions, to the noisy cheering and chanting and beating of the helpers. If there's no window at all, and no way to get out onto the roof, create an astral window in a pinch by drawing it in the air, opening it ceremoniously, and sweeping everything out. (Just please, please make sure you close it afterwards, and either remember it's there or ritually erase it. If you choose to keep it there, or if you "open" it so many times that it just starts to stay there, don't put anyone's bed under it just in case it opens up, and check on it regularly to see if it's leaking.)

Workplace Stealth Ritual

Most practioners of the magical arts, regardless of their tradition or personal creed, generally prefer to do their thing in a fairly controlled environment where they can "Do As They Will," with all the tools and trappings that this involves. Some situations that call for a spiritual solution (especially where all other practical, physical solutions have been exhausted) are not particularly ideal scenarios for the ringing of bells, waving of smudgewands, or droning of chants in obscure languages. In the post-industrial twenty-first century, the most common scenario where stealth ritual is called for may undoubtedly be the workplace.

Regardless of whether you are entombed in a cubicle in Dilbertland or chained to a workstation in a machine shop, the obstacles revolving around performing acts of magic in the workplace are the same. Whether you are out of the broomcloset to your coworkers or not, carting out the usual bells and smells would bring undesirable attention to yourself in the form of curious (or upset) onlookers getting in the way, or a barrage of rumors that could make your job unbearable.

In ceremonial magic traditions, there is the concept of the "astral temple." It was a goal of many dedicated ceremonial magicians to be so familiar with their altar tools and so mentally disciplined that the physical presence of those tools would be unnecessary, as they could be "willed" into existance astrally at any time. Don't feel bad if this is not your bag. We are both tool-using monkeys, and still manage to perform the fine art of stealth magic. Regardless of your style or tradition of casting, one thing will be certain: The seriousness of your "prep work" is going to increase significantly. After all, the art of manifesting the Will is not simply a matter of "wishing." Power has to be raised, focused, and directed toward your goal, regardless of your ability to improvise. We recommend that you pay extra attention to your preparations. For instance, if you are going to be using a substance such as a food, beverage, or oil to mark the boundaries of your workspace, take the time at home to charge it properly.

If you are going to draw symbols with your finger, practice drawing them beforehand to the point where you can recall them accurately. You can work with objects that you conceal on your body; you can bring apparently ordinary objects into your workspace; or you can create spaces in which to hide your various magical trinkets.

stealth cleansing via repelling negative energy

Breath Cleansing. For this, you want to chew or drink something with a strong herbal taste. We recommend anything menthol, such as spearmint gum; ginger beer (of the hot Jamaican variety); anything with hot pepper or lots of garlic in it, such as chips; or something like raw onion if you can stand it. It should be in your mouth as you walk around. Walk the boundaries of the space, periodically drawing in a deep breath and blowing it out in a long, directed stream of air. As you blow, imagine your breath to be that of a fiery dragon, blowing away all negativity. Then take another bite or sip or chew, and a few more steps, and do it again. Aim your breath at any area that is especially full of ugly emotions, but don't aim it straight at people's faces, please. If sound won't call attention to you, then humming or whistling while doing it adds power and focus.

Substance Cleansing. Go around the boundaries of the area, making symbols with your fingertip in order to drive off nasty vibes. Suggested substances to add to your fingertip are essential oil, liquid soap, high-proof liquor, or just water if you're worried about residues on surfaces. (Raven has managed well with Vicks, in a pinch.) Good places to lay symbols are door lintels, windows, corners, and ventilation gratings. You can use a simple circle to symbolize a shield around the area, or your initial, or a circle with the diagonal slash through it for a warding-off sign.

Tea smudge. Make a strong cup of herbal tea (you can actually do this with herbs like sage, cinnamon, ginger, or mint) and walk around your space with it. The fumes will act like a smudge.

stealth cleansing via warding off people who bring negative energy

Warding sigil. It is common in cubicles and areas around work benches to place pictures of family members, pets, pinups, or vacation places. If you mat or frame them, you can add a piece of parchment with a warding sigil in between the mat or frame and the picture.

Warding symbols. These can be taped underneath desks or chairs; just remember to take them with you if you change jobs!

Charge up a small toy or statue to act as a gargoyle to keep unwanted visitors away and place them on top of your desk, computer monitor, or workbench. Touch or fiddle with it to activate it when someone you wish to avoid is around or due to arrive.

Plant. If the environment warrants it, bring a living prickly plant into your workspace concealing a charged sigil or image of the person you wish to repel underneath or in the dirt.

Keep in mind that, in cleansing spaces that are not your own, small is better. A whole building is pretty much a lost cause for one person to attempt. Stick to a single, small room that is public, but that you frequent regularly. Also, it's rude to cleanse someone else's private space (for example, a coworker's office) without their permission.

five

Reliquaries

ANCIENT GODS IN A MODERN WORLD

• • We tend to think of ancient deities as being creatures of a simpler, more rural time when people lived in tiny villages and hardly ever saw each other, and thus as being less sophisticated than we are today. To assume this is to make a great mistake. First of all, although some deities such as Pan or Cernunnos or Artemis are more at home in the wilderness, many deities were creatures more of cities than of the countryside. Many were city patrons in ancient times, and some had cities named after them, such as Athens. Nearly all had temples or specific representatives in every major city. Today, although their official temples may be few and far between, there are many areas that they still claim, quietly, in ways we don't tend to notice.

(Over the following pages, we'll list off a lot of gods and goddesses, and where to go in order to find and get in touch with them. We don't have the space to discuss each one and their various myths in detail;

if you don't recognize a deity and they sound interesting, please do your own research. We apologize ahead of time for the cursory nature of this discussion, both to our readers and our gods.)

Before we start listing, we'll tell you what the point to all this is. It's part of using the magic of Place to invoke a deity for help or worship. All you'll need to do is leave an offering for them in the places that they have affinities for, along with a spoken or unspoken request, or perhaps just a word of appreciation. The offerings themselves can be something representing their major attributes, or something they might have liked to eat or drink; in a pinch, a small picture or something associated with that deity (like a woodland scene for Cernunnos), rolled up, will work.

If you work in an industry or building that is the special provenance of a particular god, it's a good thing to make regular offerings to them, and perhaps set up a discreet altar somewhere on the site.

Since we mentioned Athens, we'll start with Athena. Patron of wisdom and learning, the best place to invoke her is a college campus, preferably closer to its main park or administrative center than to its rowdiest dorms. Libraries, too, are sacred to Athena, and also to Thoth, the Egyptian God of Writing.

Zeus, or Odin in his capacity of king, or any other law-giving head god, can be found in the local town or city hall, or state capitol building. The bigger the political sway of the building, the better. His wife Hera, Goddess of Marriage, has as her special places marital counseling centers, marriage "consultants," bridal shops, and anywhere associated with the wedding industry. The best place to leave an offering to her, however, is somewhere that a wedding has just been performed.

Apollo and any other sun gods may be left offerings in bright, sunny places, especially deserts, if you have one around. Also, offerings to solar deities such as Horus and Helios and Ra may be attached to the corners of solar PV panels. If you don't have very many of them in your town, you should. If you have an apartment with a flat roof that you can get to, or a balcony high in the air, make a sun out of tinfoil, inscribe your wish on it with a pen that's run out of ink (they make great styluses), and leave it laying flat and facing upward so that it reflects the sun's rays for a whole day. (Obviously, don't do this on an overcast day.)

Apollo, as God of Music, can also be propitiated in record stores, or even by playing music in your own home. However, the serene and conservative Apollo is not much interested in rock or rap or hip-hop. Put on some classical music, or he'll frown. He is most often given offerings for the gift of a clear intellect and studying ability.

Artemis, although more of a forest deity, is still found in many city places today. Women's shelters, women's health clinics, and feminist political centers are sacred to her. Demeter's energy can be found in such places as child-care centers, grocery stores, and especially those food baskets in grocery stores that encourage you to donate canned food for the homeless. This is a very good way of propitiating Demeter if, for instance, you'd like her help in conceiving a child.

Actually, the grocery store is a good place to make an offering to any fertility goddess, such as Gaea, Freya, or Demeter—especially the produce section. I suspect that they especially appreciate small mom-and-pop, fruit-stand-type places; actually buying something from her unwitting priest/esses is a good way to seal the magic.

Kwan Yin, Goddess of Mercy and Compassion, is also found at soup kitchens, and at the Goodwill and Salvation Army stores where clothing is available for low-income folk. An offering made to her there can bring in some used item you've been waiting for, although it might be better to propitiate Skor (see next chapter).

Hestia is a Domestic Hearth Goddess, and her sacred place is the flame at the hearth of any home. Don't have a fireplace in your apartment? You do have a furnace in the building, and if there's a gas stove, you have a pilot light, the modern version of the ever-burning flame. That's where you burn an offering to her.

Dionysus, God of Wine, Dance, and Altered States, has two distinct forms. The earlier Dionysus was a feminine, castrated, cross-dressing deity who had rulership of shamanic altered states, wild dancing, and drink and drugs. His later Roman incarnation, Bacchus, was a rowdy, masculine, bearded, merry God of Wine who was actually absorbed from the Roman God Liber, meaning "liberty." Both and either can be propitiated by pouring out some alcohol, and offerings can be left for them in and around liquor stores or bars. Some city folk of Italian descent will grow grapevines in their yards, and one can discreetly hang a gold coin (it can be fake) among the vines as an offering. Dionysus has special rulership in drag bars, movie theaters, and stage theaters. Another of his constantly moving sacred sites is the kind of rock concert that encourages lots of dancing and altered states; Joseph Campbell commented that the closest thing the modern era had to a Dionysian revel was a Grateful Dead concert. Bacchus appears more in other mainstream sorts of bars, especially ones with lots of good fellowship.

Warrior gods such as Ares/Mars have their sacred sites in such places as military recruiting stations or bases, martial arts schools, and gyms. Apollo also likes gyms, as they are a place to improve yourself, as does the Afro-Caribbean Fire Orisha Shango. Appropriate offerings are beer and spicy foods. We find hot-chili tortilla chips work well. Offering them to your fellow gym-goers in a warrior god's name will get you points on several fronts.

The Egyptian Warrior Goddess Sekhmet prefers stone lions and lionesses as her offering places. Do not do it at the zoo; she is offended by caged lions and other great cats.

Aphrodite, Oshun, Ishtar, and any of the love goddesses have rulership over such obvious places as dating services and singles' bars, but the best place to leave an offering to them is someplace that is known as the local Lover's Lane. If you'd lay money that people go there to make out, that's her sacred place. Another even better thing is to go to a strip bar. The girls working there may not know it, but they are the heiresses of the sacred harlots of ancient times, whose Dance of the Hours, the Hora, came down to us as the word "whore." Give them money, and do it in such a way as to seem respectful and worshipful. Refer to a dancer who approaches you as

"Lady" or "Goddess," and pay her, and ask nothing of her, and leave. In such a way does magic transform the world.

The other inheritors of the Love Goddess's sacred tradition are ladies of the evening. Since giving them money might be seen as suspect by possible police onlookers, the best thing to do is to give them other gifts and offerings, such as food or small bottles of wine, in their place as the Goddess's unwitting servants. You can keep the contact brief if you like, and explain your behavior or not as you choose, but the important thing is that you ask nothing of them for your gift. The Love Goddess will see and approve, and she's who you're asking things of, at any rate.

Vocational schools are sacred to Ptah, the Egyptian God of Work. Ditto apprenticeship programs. His symbol is the scarab beetle; you can paste a cutout scarab on the wall of a vo-tech school (near the ceiling—the scarab rolls the sun along) and he'll be pleased and help your endeavor. On the other hand, talk to Prometheus if it's labor unions you hang around, or for that matter any civil rights activist organization. Make a paper chain, label it with the unfair behavior that is binding you, tear it in two, and leave the pieces in some hidden place in their building.

To find any of the smith gods, such as Hephaestus, Volund, or possibly Brigid, trot down to your nearest machinist's shop or auto mechanic's garage. Brigid herself, as Goddess not only of Fire and Steel but of Poetry and Inspiration, has a particular affinity with space travel, and if you actually have somewhere NASA-like in your town, leave her something special.

Planetariums are sacred to Nuit/Nut, the Star Goddess, in the dust of whose feet are the hosts of heaven. On the other hand, the science museums to which they are usually attached are more Athena's territory.

Saturn, the dour old God of Time and Karma, has a special place at the IRS. Anything to do with tax collection is his territory. Leaving offerings outside the door of the local IRS building is a good way to get him on your side. Ask him to send you a good accountant, or to overlook your own accounting foibles this time.

Thor, the Norse God of Thunder and Lightning, will find it amusing if you leave an offering at the gates of the local power company. He also likes trains, because they are loud and thundering, and you can leave an offering on the tracks. Please be careful in both cases.

Hermes/Mercury, God of Travelers, is best invoked either at the bus station or the airport. He is also a patron of taxi drivers; if you overtip one and say it's for Hermes, He'll appreciate it.

The Egyptian Goddess Isis is a healer and the patron of physicians; make offerings to her at doctors' offices, hospitals, and medical schools, usually for healing.

Bast, the Egyptian Cat Goddess, has as her special place the ASPCA, or any place that rescues cats (of course). Give her cans of cat food, or nice, fresh fish bits. She can help you find lost cats.

The Hindu deity Sarasvati, as well as the Greek Muses, can be found at art schools, and stores that sell arts and crafts materials. Invoke them for artist's block.

Her cousin Lakshmi, the Hindu Goddess of Good Fortune, loves fountains. Throw in coins—the bigger and more ornate the fountain, the better.

The Afro-Caribbean Orisha Oya, as well as being a lady of storms and death, is protector of the marketplace, and can be invoked anywhere there is an open market, or a store with the name "market" on it. Give her some red wine, and suck the breath into your lungs very fast nine times.

Ogoun, the Afro-Caribbean hunter deity, is associated with the police, and offerings to him can be left at the police station. The archangel St. Michael is the actual patron saint of policemen, and you can talk to him there too. You might make such offerings to ask that the eyes of the law not turn to you, to help them catch a wrongdoer, and to keep the local police fair, just, and objective.

The Norse God Heimdall, the guardian of the gateway of Asgard, is the patron of all security guards and doormen. Get his attention by bringing one an offering, perhaps of chocolate or something else tempting like that.

Botanical gardens and flower shops are the provenance of Flora/Kore, the spring maiden, lady of new life. She can be asked for help when recovering from a death or trauma, or in recovery from some addiction, as she gives you a new lease on life.

In terms of sea gods, well, the best place to leave an offering for them is at the seaside. In fact, all over the world, people leave offerings to the various sea deities by creating small altars on the beach at low tide with offerings of food, drink, and flowers, usually in seashells, and when the waters rise, they are swept away. The Afro-Caribbean Sea Goddess Yemaya is revered this way on the summer solstice all over coastal South America. Aquariums and sea wildlife preserves are good places to leave offerings as well. (Please do not leave man-made, nonorganic substances such as wrappers or plastic bags in reach of the animals; this will endanger them.) Poseidon, as a god associated with earthquakes, ought to be regularly propitiated by people on the West Coast.

Of course, this only works if you actually live on the coast. If, for whatever reason, you wish to propitiate sea gods and you live in the middle of a continent, you might have to make a symbolic ocean. This can be done two ways. You can make a big bowl (wok-size, for instance) of salt water, add some small pieces of seaweed and a few tiny dried fishes (sort of like a sea stew; we get dried fishes at the local Korean grocery), and then sink a tiny, pebble-sized stone with a symbol of your wish drawn on it into the bowl, and leave it for a while. Flush the "stew" down the toilet when you're done—water to water. Or you can create a collage of sea stuff—magazine pictures of fishes in their natural habitat, ocean pictures, and so on—and put it on your wall, and meditate on it. Science mags often have good sea articles with fish pictures.

The death gods are a special case and they have a whole section of the city to themselves, to be covered in a different chapter. (See chapter 14, Into the Depths.) However, in their above-ground aspects, there is the city morgue and the cemeteries.

One of the most ambivalent divine figures you'll see on the street is the red-clad old man who invades almost every space come

Yuletide: Santa Claus. We are firmly of the opinion that Santa is an amalgam of elder gods, come back to claim Yule for his own. He is akin to the red-clad Holly King, who defeats the Oak King every spring and grows old by Yule, to give over his place to the new Sun Child; and to the Russian Father Frost who is the embodiment of winter, along with the Frost King. His legions of elves associate him with the Faery King, and astrologically he is associated with Jupiter, the Giver of Abundance. Some have also seen him as Odin, passing out seedlings of his World Tree. At any rate, he is the God of Yule, and no modern creation. Leaving offerings at the feet of Santa figures in order for him to grant you abundance throughout the coming year is appropriate. Some folk feel that tossing a coin into the cauldron of the many live stand-in Santas ringing their bells about town will do the same thing, if the will behind it is focused. Others would prefer not to donate to those organizations for religious reasons. The choice is up to you.

six

Modernism

THE URBAN TRIPLE DEITIES

The Triple Urban Goddess

The Urban Goddess of America has three faces of great power: by name Squat, Skor, and Skram. Each of them is invaluable for the urban primitive to call on in times of need and, like all deities, she will answer more often when called more often.

squat

Squat is a big goddess. A very, very big goddess. Picture her as weighing in at over three hundred pounds of warm, round, abundant, billowing flesh. Her personality is just as warm and merry and abundant as her figure, and a good thing too, for Squat is the Goddess of Parking Spaces.

To invoke her, you have to start early—before you even get to wherever you're going, start calling on her and telling dirty jokes. She really loves dirty jokes, the worse the better. We're told she especially enjoys nun jokes. If she is amused by your offering,

squat

she will squat on a parking space and hold it for you until you arrive, fending off intruders with her considerable divine bulk.

If no one is feeling inspired to tell dirty jokes, bad doggerel said in her honor will work. One of our classic favorites goes, "O great and bounteous Squat, we like you a lot, we really think you're hot, oh, please, give us a parking spot!" and so on, in that vein. Use blatant and obvious toadying. She likes that kind of thing.

Squat is also invoked in order to find housing, as that is considered a place to park yourself. This calls for more elaborate invocation, such as writing dirty jokes on bathroom walls or subway posters or perhaps leafleting them on the street. Intoning them loudly in crowded elevators could work as well. Remember, you are entertainment for her. Make it good and she'll work with you, but you'd better provide her some belly laughs at your expense in return.

As an urban primitive, your living space is especially important to you in terms of a safe haven. Pay attention to the wards around your house, and remember the toilet brush ritual. (See chapters on Defenses and Migration.)

skor

Skor, the second face of the Triple Urban Goddess, is the Goddess of Yard Sales, Flea Markets, and especially Trashpicking. Whatever you need in terms of physical objects, Skor will find it for you. She appears at first glance to be a bedraggled bag lady, sifting through garbage, but if you bother to draw close to her, you will see her great beauty shining through. And so it is with her gifts. If you tell Skor what you need, she'll try to provide it for you. It may take a few weeks or months to get someone to throw it out in your path, or it may be a matter of hours, but she'll take care of it. She appreciates being called on, and the more you call on her, the quicker she'll respond. We've had amazing luck getting what we want from the city's discards after having worked with Skor for a few years.

skor

There are a variety of things that sweet Skor likes. First, when you find something good on one of her sacred curbsides, remember to yell "Skor!" in thanks. When you have something you don't want but that still has use or wear in it, put it out in a heavily trashpicked area so that Skor can make use of it and send it where it needs to go. For a quick invocation to her, throw a few pennies onto the sidewalk and ask for her help. We like to say a little rhyme in thanks as we haul something away: "Skor is great, Skor is cute, and we thank her for the loot, rah rah Skor!"

As a city dweller, unless you have enough money to buy what you want when you need it—and most urban primitives don't—trashpicking is a skill that you should learn, and quickly. Learn the trash days in your neighborhood, and learn them in wealthier neighborhoods too. Make time during the week to do rounds, especially if you can bring either a car or an easily pulled cart, such as a luggage cart or wagon, for the bigger items.

If you live in a city with one or more four-year colleges, it would be well worth your time to stop in and pick up an academic calendar. The trashpicking will be particularly good at the end of each semester, approximately from the last week of classes through graduation day. Cultivating the friendship of people who work in the dorms can also give you access to a semester-end supply of tiny refrigerators and lumber previously used to make lofts and bookshelves. For more frequent trashpicking during the school year, there's no better place for little gifts and barely-used athletic footwear (and much more) than the dumpsters behind rich kids' Greek houses. The sororities in particular tend to tire of things and toss them with reckless abandon.

skram

Skram, the third member of the Urban Goddess trinity, is the goddess who tells you when not to be there. Not much is known about Skram, for she comes and goes in quick moments, and doesn't leave

skram

much except her calling card, which is a strong feeling in the depths of your gut. You know Skram's presence when you get that almost claustrophobic feeling of needing to leave, that magnet between your shoulder blades yanking you toward the door. Skram is always right. If you don't leave when she calls, disaster will ensue. Of course, not all of your fears and worries are the call of Skram, and it takes practice and attention to separate your own random internal phobias from her prescient awareness.

When Skram calls you, something is going to happen that it would be better for you not to be present for. The cop outside may be coming toward your illegally parked vehicle; your angry ex-lover may be about to walk in the other door of the store; the sullen guy in line at McDonald's may be about to snap and go postal. Skram rarely gives details, just an all-points bulletin to evacuate the area as soon as possible.

You don't invoke Skram; she calls you. You don't make offerings to Skram; what pleases her the most is when you react to her calls instead of simply dismissing them. The more you pay attention to her and do what she asks, the more often she'll warn you, and the clearer the warnings will be. The more you ignore her, the less she'll waste her time with you, until she no longer bothers at all. Working with Skram can help develop your internal psychic sensitivities; by teaching you to listen when she grabs your inner bell and rings it, she accustoms you to using it yourself.

The Triple Urban God

Equal time! The Triple Urban God is the counterpart to the Triple Urban Goddess, although we don't want to speculate what their actual relationships are, as that would be an invasion of privacy and we'd probably get it all wrong anyway. His three faces are Slick, Screw, and Sarge, all of which are just as useful to the urban primitive.

SEAN PETRIN

slick

slick

He's got greasy hair, greasy smile
He says, "Lord, this must be
my destination."

JOHN MELLENCAMP, "PINK HOUSES"

Slick is a deity we all love to hate when we come up against him, or against someone who has successfully invoked him. There are people out there who are practically possessed by Slick, usually salesmen and people in the advertising business, and it is true that he is the most capricious of all six of these divine faces. There's no guarantee that he'll help you if you ask, and even if you've been a devoted disciple of his for twenty years, there's no guarantee that he'll help you tomorrow.

Slick gives the gift of fast-talking and thinking. He helps you slide out of a situation with as little conflict, confrontation, and penalty as possible. When he blesses you, the right things to say just slide out of your mouth, and you'll see the characteristic glazed expression on the face of the other person, who is then seized and tamed by the power of Slick's voice moving through you. People believe what Slick says, religiously. Slick is a good guy, a smart guy, a guy who makes sense, and so will you as far as they are concerned. They will also feel their own sense of self-worth expanding, as they realize how intelligent they are to listen to and understand the deep meaning of Slick's words. It doesn't matter if those words are total nonsense; it's the magic, not the meaning, that makes the difference. It's a heady power, to say the least.

Although Slick can get you out of a lot of trouble by way of his vocal tranquilizers, there's a danger involved. Not only can he let you down when you're most expecting his help, but if you invoke him too frequently he can start using you as his very own ventriloquist's dummy, even when you didn't ask for it or want it. Your mouth will open, and you'll say things you didn't expect, and it'll be Slick talking, not you . . . and before you know it, you aren't able to speak your own honest mind anymore, because Slick owns your

SEAN PETRIN

screw

mouth. So the idea is moderation. Don't call on him except in emergencies, and placate him well so that he won't get any ideas about moving in.

Slick is invoked by using anything slippery, such as satin, vinyl, car enamel, or mayonnaise. Man-made substances are the best. Rub them, and ask for help. If it's something non-fabric, and you can spit on it and rub it in, so much the better. The ultimate spell to invoke Slick is to put a dab of hair gel in your hair. If it works and he helps you out, placate him afterwards by polishing something until it shines. It doesn't have to be something of yours; in fact, the more people that will see it, the better.

screw

Screw, as you might imagine, gets you laid. The second face of the Triple Urban God, Screw has many faces, all of them devastatingly handsome and sexy. He always smells great, and his hair is always perfect. He's not in charge of romance or love, just itch-scratching. He can't guarantee that the encounter will last more than the night, if that, but if you're willing to settle for a wild, ephemeral time, he can come up with the goods.

Screw's ritual items are mostly made of latex. Tie three knots in a condom, dental dam, or latex glove and hang it somewhere public, like the spike of a chain-link fence. Ask for what you want, and he'll deliver. It helps, of course, if you manage to bathe and wear clean clothing and not act like a jerk; Screw is good, but don't make his job any harder than it already is. It also helps if you actually leave the house and make contact with human beings, unless you really want a torrid one-afternoon stand with the meter reader.

Screw is amiable and easygoing, the least offendable of the Urban Gods. He's always up for a party, so it's okay to ask for his help again and again, but you'll need to make regular offerings to him if you get his help a lot. This consists of giving said latex goodies away to other people—friends, lovers, strangers on the street. Don't try to make judgments about who might or might not have a use for

sarge

them. Just give them away. People may think they won't need them, and then the moment may arise suddenly, without warning, and it's good to have something tucked away just in case.

Screw is a proponent of safe, casual sex. Death is a bummer, and gets him down. So does monogamy, or celibacy, or any of that. Just be responsible and have a good time, he says. His morality is not that of many—or most—people, and it doesn't have to be yours, either, to contact him; he doesn't really care what you do with the rest of your life, and he doesn't really care what you think of his values, either. He isn't interested in judging your sexual preferences, although if you ask him to get you laid, you'd best specify what you want or he might just idly reach into his grab bag and see what's at hand.

sarge

Sarge, the third face of the Triple Urban God, is the least praised of all the urban deities, yet when you need him, you *really* need him. Sarge is the one who gets you off your ass and gives you the motivation to do some important thing that you really hate to think about. He can be pictured as a middle-aged man with a crew cut and fatigues, yelling something like, "Moveitmoveitmoveit! All right, soldier, up off your tush and get going! Come on, I've seen dead bodies with more action than you! Make some tracks or I'll set fire to your shoes!" And so forth. Sarge never bothers you on his own; if you really want that badly to procrastinate until your life is a shambles, he'll simply avoid you in disgust. You can call on him at any time, simply by asking, and he'll do his best to motivate you, until you either get the job done or he gives up in frustration over your laziness or cowardice.

Sarge can help you to face the DMV, call the landlord, fix the busted pipe, or trudge on down to the unemployment office. Support and hand-holding are not his forte; if that's what you want, try other, more nurturing deities first. Sarge is the last resort, when all other, more positive, options have failed, and you know deep down that the only thing that's going to get you through this unpleasant task is constant mental badgering.

Sarge can also be invoked and sent off to bother other people for you, if they're procrastinating or late. One Sarge story we know involves a witch who was waiting for a truck from the junkyard to deliver a transmission to the house. The transmission had already been delivered the night before, but to the wrong house. The junkyard owner assured our friend that the truck driver who'd erred would correct the mistake, and that it would be there by noon. When noon came and went with no sign of the errant driver, she decided to invoke Sarge. She asked mentally for his help, and pictured someone looking vaguely like Sergeant Bilko leaning into the slack face of the truck driver, invisibly haranguing him until he stopped whatever he was doing and got the job done. Soon afterwards, he arrived, appearing nervous and harassed and looking over his shoulder rather frequently, and the transmission was delivered.

You can use this technique on others, although you should be careful; Sarge really does want to help people in his own way, and if he sees that they're really overworked and there's no way they can go any faster, he'll leave them alone and report this back to you. What he wants in return is simply to be thanked, sincerely. Let him know that his efforts are appreciated, even when he can't help. Don't ever take him for granted, and don't act as though you're afraid of him. He can be a useful friend in times of depression and lethargy.

Some people have claimed that the Urban Gods correspond to astrological influences (i.e., Squat being lunar, Skor Jupiterian, Scram Uranian, Slick Mercurial, Screw Venusian, and Sarge Saturnian); others have claimed that they are simply some of the old gods wearing modern costumes, and associate Screw with Krishna, Slick with Hermes, and so forth. We, the authors, are not going to assume that we know so much about them as to be able to verify or disprove these facts. Just keep in mind that pole-vaulting to conclusions often leaves one squashed flat on a mat, and that too much syncretism done on a stomach empty of sufficient facts tends to lead to spiritual indigestion. In other words, nothing's ever as simple as you think it is.

seven

Territory

THE ELEMENTS OF PLACE

"It occurs to me that certain plants, especially trees, are tied into the consciousness and local spirits of a place. Here in Nashville we have cedars. My Gods, do we have cedars! To the degree that one of the suburbs is named Lebanon, and a few miles outside that, Cedars of Lebanon State Park. I have three of them in my yard, and one is a regular dedication spot—the area around its base is where we put the occasional dead beetle and butterfly, the mice and birds that the cats bring in, and the other dead creatures that turn up about the property, as offerings to Hecate. Who thinks of Atlanta without thinking of peach trees? Or Miami and palms, or Tucson and the majestic saguaro cacti? Tying into the energies of these quiet, standing guardians of the locale can be a powerful and gratifying experience.

"My favorite small magic in the city is the magic of Place. Just as the rocks, holes, trees, hills, and streams of the rural countryside each have their own spirit and character, the landscape of the city possesses these things as well. I try to get to know the places I frequent—the art supply shop, the cappuccino bar at the local bookstore, the Italian cheap-eats place, the railroad track between my house and the grocery store walking distance away, the park at the heart of the city with its duck pond, its playgrounds, and its full-scale reproduction of the Parthenon with the massive Athena statue within.

"I know the people and the animals that frequent these places, by name and face and aura—Prissy, the poodle who owns the man who owns the art store and keeps my children entertained when we're there; the robins and pigeons around the railroad track; the sweet and gentle old lady who clerks at the grocery store and pouts if I don't notice her and get in her line. I can feel a sense of recognition and welcome from certain stores and restaurants even before I step on the property; the place itself knows and welcomes me, and I appreciate its welcome. When one builds a relationship with places, and sees and feels the energy there, living in the city can be a rich and gratifying experience—hardly a lonely wandering among dead concrete and steel."

Beth Harper, Nashville Witch

• • The first point in dealing with the elements of place is, literally, dealing with the elements. Elemental spirits will naturally be drawn to certain areas, and these will be the best place to find them. The spirits of Earth, Air, Fire, and Water are just as present in urban areas as they are in the wild; after all, everything is made from them. Don't believe us? Think it's just all superstition, that the "real" elements are things like oxygen and helium and plutonium? Consider that when early people separated all things in combinations of these "elements," they were actually trying to describe what scientists today refer to as states of matter—solid, liquid, and gas (Earth, Water, and

Air), with Fire representing the only other thing that something can be: energy. Everything is either matter or energy, so far as we know, and it does seem to fall into these categories, although we'll be interested to see the day when someone brings home a coffee can of "dark matter" to play with. One could also make a case that the four great forces of physics fit fairly neatly into the elemental mold as well—gravity is earthy (of course!); electromagnetism is fiery; the strong force is like unto water, which brings together; and the weak force is like unto air, which separates us. The point, however, is that belief in magic does not preclude belief in science, or vice versa.

So: On to the elements.

The Elements

air

Air is the element of the breath, the mind, words, communication, thinking, and song. It rules spring, dawn, the direction of the east, the sense of smell and, of course, the wind. In scientific terms, it is the matter form of gas, and is associated symbolically with the "weak force" of physics. Its symbols are knives and blades, like the mind that analyzes and cuts things apart, and fans, fluttery ribbons, and so on. One good place to find the spirits of Air is on the phone lines. They travel back and forth, using these lines (NOT the power lines; those are reserved for the Fire spirits) and listening to our conversations. To summon an Air elemental, pick up the phone, press the star or asterisk key (*), and sing three notes into the phone. Then speak your needs and hang up. Air spirits make great messengers, communicating via hunches, stray thoughts, and sudden reminders. Since most of us have phones and use them, we're putting ourselves in their hands on a daily basis, and they should be able to deliver your message to someone the second they pick up the phone and hear that dial tone. Make sure that you visualize the recipient clearly when you state your message, so that there's no question of where it needs to go. Air elementals are somewhat forgetful and capricious; some might even say scatterbrained. Yes, cordless phones work just as well; the Air elementals hear everything that goes through the air.

As you might expect, modems are also the playgrounds of these mischievous sprites, and we've had luck asking them to get someone to check their email and find a message from us. We simply did the above maneuver with the phone to warn them, and then unplugged the phone, plugged in the modem, and sent the message. They can also be asked to provide an "escort" to particularly important or sensitive data that is going over the phone lines via modem. Can they help you in cyberspace? Not very much; they are rather limited in their focus and cyberspace is too complex for them. We suspect a new breed of spirit will evolve to take up residence in cyberspace, or an old one will discover it and move in. But Air spirits are better used for simple, easy tasks that don't require a lot of heavy analytical and logical thought.

Anything that produces a clear tone will attract Air elementals, such as pitchpipes, tuning forks, or synthesizers. They also like wind chimes to play with as toys; if you want to make friends with Air spirits, put up a bunch of wind chimes outside your door, as if you were leaving catnip-stuffed toy mice for the cats. They love music, too; you can call them in your car by rolling the windows down, driving fast, and playing your stereo loudly. They'll follow out of curiosity and pleasure. Music makes a good offering to them, as does incense and perfume sprayed into the air.

Gas lines also carry Air elementals, but we hope we don't have to tell you how dangerous gas can be. Since natural gas is flammable, an anti-gas spell in your house should placate both Air and Fire elementals (see below).

In high buildings, on several-story roofs, and observation platforms, you can connect with the spirit of the wind, the biggest Air elemental of all. It will speak to you there, because your presence, outside and listening at that high level, is unusual among humans and attracts its attention. Connecting with this spirit can bring great changes and intellectual growth. It especially likes to be sung to, even if you aren't a great singer. The spirit of the wind has many powers, including that of objectivity, the high sight and the long view, and farseeing. It can tell you what's happening in the city, or at least what it sees from its high vantage point. It can purify you of cluttering feelings and help you gain objectivity toward heavy emotional problems. It will probably not offer a solution to a problem so much as clear your head and point you in the right direction to find the answer yourself.

fire

Fire is the element of the will, the vital life force, and passion of any kind, be it love, rage, or obsession. It rules summer, high noon, the direction of the south, the sense of sight, and all forms of energy that produce heat or burn calories. In scientific terms, it is associated with energy as opposed to matter, and associated symbolically with the force of electromagnetism in physics. Its symbol is the wand or staff, which was originally a torch. Some say that the wand is Fire's symbol because the energy is supposed to be channeled through it; well, in the city, you can take that metaphor one step further and make your "wand" out of an actual conducting metal. Fire spirits travel around using the power lines the way that Air spirits use the phone lines. A power station is the strongest possible place to visit Fire spirits; usually they're surrounded by high chainlink fences, which is a very good idea as they're dangerous places, and so are Fire elementals. Be respectful of Fire spirits; stand outside that power station, behind the fence, and talk to them in a quiet, reasonable tone of voice so as not to stir them up. They are glad to do you favors, but they have a tendency to do them in the most drastic and dramatic way possible—for example, all the times that we know of when someone's asked a Fire deity or spirit to bring them money, some terrible disaster occurs (like a car accident or a building burning down) for which they are ultimately paid an insurance settlement. You can ask them to give you energy if you are tired and depressed all the time, but be careful to preserve that energy carefully and not "burn out." Asking Fire spirits to help you with your love life will bring passion into it, as well as storms and obsession. If that sort of thing is right up your alley, great. If you'd rather have a quiet, peaceful, affectionate relationship without a lot of argument, talk to the Water guys.

We do not suggest that you play too much with the power lines that ride over your streets, as this can too easily result in injury. You can—carefully—utilize the Fire spirits' entry into your home, namely the electric plugs in the wall, but not by sticking dangerous items into them. A friend we know uses a red-tinted light bulb that he plugs into the wall, turns out the lights so that it's the only source of illumination, and then speaks to them. He says that if you do this often enough, they'll get the idea that this bulb is your way of calling them. However, calling Fire spirits into your home is dangerous at best, as they might decide to stay and play unsafely, and they really don't care if they burn down your house. Better to do the invoking outside, in an empty lot. Use a portable battery and plug your "calling item," like a special light, into it.

Fire spirits were traditionally called with candles, and of course you can do this too. Keep in mind that candles should not be left unattended, and that in a small, closed space with no ventilation they may breathe all your air for you. If you work with them outside, put them in empty mayonnaise jars or the like. Never wax a candle directly onto the street; it may be made of inflammable asphalt, but there's all sorts of flammable dust and trash around it that could blow in and catch. Flicking on a lighter, such as one does at rock concerts, and holding it high will definitely get their attention. Smoking a cigarette or something else and making circles with the smoke will work as well, for lots of things as well as invoking Fire spirits. Be aware that whenever you inhale smoke, you bring them into your body. If you are addicted to smoking, they own you. Becoming addicted to smoking is a tacit agreement to become, eventually, a sacrifice for them. They will give you that fire energy in return, until you burn out like a match. Make your own choices, but remember that the smoking addiction "burning out" death is both inevitable and fairly nasty.

Other fire spells, more showy and dangerous, are done with gasoline, oil, or alcohol. A design is traced on the surface of an object, and then it's set on fire. The idea is that the flammable stuff burns away and the fire goes on without lighting the object. Frankly, we think that gasoline and oil are just too dangerous to use; stick with alcohol and make sure that the surface is wet before messing with this. We've done the alcohol version successfully on all sorts of things, including human beings. Alcohol flame is blue and burns with a lower heat than normal; it won't burn living flesh for the few seconds it's alight, especially if that flesh is thoroughly wet down first. It will, however, singe all the hair off, and this is not something to do on the face or head, or anywhere that the head hair could catch fire. Our suggestions are *(a)* to use the back of the hand or the chest, and *(b)* to find someone who can show you how to do it properly. Done right and safely, it is a whopper of a protection spell on whomever receives it. **However, please use a great deal of caution! Fire can spread and kill. Take many safety precautions and consult someone experienced first.**

If there's too much fire in your life—if you're embroiled, for example, in an angry breakup or messy divorce, if you find yourself or your loved ones on edge, with chips on their shoulders and blowing their tops too often, build an altar around the anti-fire devices found on every street corner: fire hydrants. Make them into a magical item by drawing on them with colored chalk, placing stickers on them (hearts, flowers, and other peaceful symbols work well), or surrounding them with a ring of fresh earth, small stones, bits of bottle glass, or other grounding/cooling items. Ask the spirits of Fire to take a vacation from your life for a while, but reassure them that you really do value them and you'll want them back later; you just feel too "scorched" right now. If a hydrant doesn't seem big enough, do it in front of the local fire station.

water

Water is the element of the heart and emotions, love and hate, and is linked to the moon, which controls its tides. It is traditionally associated with autumn, evening, the direction of the west, the sense of taste, and all nonflammable liquids, including your own blood, sweat, tears, and saliva. Scientifically, it is associated with the matter form of liquid, and associated symbolically with the strong force of physics. Water rules the emotions, the feelings, the irrational. It flows, rushes, drowns, soothes. It gives when struck, unharmed, and then closes around what strikes it. It is as all-consuming as love and despair.

The spirits of Water are equally elusive; they caress you sensuously one moment, then slip away when you try to close your hand or awareness over them. They are propitiated for reasons of healing emotion—to wash away the pain of loss, the bad breakup, the death of a loved one, the dull depression of an unfulfilled life. They can also be propitiated for practical reasons, such as preventing house fires. Water spirits travel through—you guessed it—the plumbing. They rule the sewer system and the pipes, and every faucet in your house is an entry point to them. All you have to do to talk to them is to turn on the biggest faucet in the house, probably the bathtub. Plug up the tub and let the water pour down. Water spirits speak in running water, and the stronger the rush, the louder their words. Ask for what you want and then listen to see if you can hear an answer. If you have a shower, let it pour down and fill the tub while you sit under it, letting them touch you as you listen.

A good spell to do in order to get rid of a problem, especially if it's related to emotional difficulties, such as an addiction, is this: Draw a symbol of your problem in the bottom of your bathtub with some semiliquid material, such as washable paint or ketchup or chocolate syrup. Turn on the shower and let it run down the drain.

(Hint: Make sure the drain is completely clear and the tub empties easily before trying this, or the tub will fill and create a messy ring, which is not only a bad omen but a bitch to clean up.) If, instead of getting rid of something, you want to bring a certain emotional element into your life, such as, say, love or happiness, then go ahead and plug the drain and draw a bath, letting the symbol dissolve. For this, you'll probably want to make the symbol in liquid soap, or bath salts, or essential oil, or something else you can stand to sit in. Soak in your need for a long time, and then let the bath water out. The Water spirits will take care of it for you.

Any running water will work to talk to the Water spirits, including the sewers, which are their highways. You can drop a small piece of paper with your wish, folded or crumpled tightly, into a storm drain or a river. If you know that there will be a big rainstorm tomorrow, go out the day or night before and write your will on the sidewalk with chalk. The rain spirits, which are the same water spirits that run out your faucet, only on the high end of their circular migration, will read it and wash it away.

earth

Earth is the element of the body, the physical senses, and the physical world. It is traditionally associated with winter, nighttime, evening, the direction of north, and the sense of touch. Scientifically, it is the matter form of solids, and associated symbolically with the force of gravity in physics. Earth is anything you can see and touch and have to deal with on a daily basis, from the health of your body to the rent you pay for your shelter to the food you eat. Earth spells are generally practical and short-term in nature, and have to do with basic survival—get me money and/or a job, get me a place to live, get me food, keep me stable and focused and on track.

Any patch of dirt will do for Earth spells, no matter how barren, although actual greenery helps. By that we mean weeds as well as flowers and trees; in fact weeds are often very strong magically, as they must be especially tenacious in order to survive in the city. (See Native Flora, chapter 19.) Sand is also an Earth element item, and stone, any stone. Even cement and asphalt. Yes, they are chopped up and re-formed, but it's all still rock. Sometimes the layers of cement and asphalt seem to muffle the response of the Earth, but She is still there, and She is present in every crack where a bit of green is growing up through the armor.

Earth spirits are slow and often seem sluggish to us—it's just that they live at a different rate, much slower than us, and so take longer to respond to our ephemeral, hurried calls. They are best invoked with bodily functions and fluids; mixing a bit of your saliva or other bodily fluid (we'll leave it up to your discretion) with a bit of earth is one way. Another is to close your eyes and press against the ground with both your hands, and your feet too, if you can. Sit down if possible, and feel your weight. Be very aware of the ground beneath you, how it holds you up, how gravity draws you to it in an inexorable embrace. At the same time, notice your body; feel it as solidly as you feel the ground, feel the two as one. Then ask for what you want. Don't say, "I want money." Say, "I need to shelter my body, and feed it, and give it good things." Imagine the nice things you'll do for your body—the taste of food from a fine restaurant, the texture of nice clothing, the exhilarating feel of a gym workout, and so on. Imagine these tactile images vibrating down through the ground and catching the attention of the slow-moving, earth-colored spirits.

The best and easiest thing that they can grant you is simple emotional stability. Their nature is patient and not easily ruffled, and if you are prone to nerves you should strongly consider making friends with them. Speak slowly when you talk to them. Take deep, slow breaths and be aware of your heartbeat. They can also be used to immobilize something that is bothering you—bad gossip, perhaps (don't make it personal, just do a spell to stop the gossip), or paranoias and anxieties and phobias. Draw a symbol on something, or pick up a small stone and hold it while picturing the problem, and then bury it, asking the Earth spirits to hold it for you for a while. Considering that, for them, "a while" may be long after you've died and gone on to another existence, it's a good way to imprison difficulties. Make sure you remember where you buried it, though, especially if there's any tiny chance that you might ever want to release it.

Elemental Prevarication

Now that you've just read our nice little lists of rulerships and synthesisms, we're going to throw a monkey wrench into the whole thing. The directions, times of day, seasons, and so forth that are traditionally associated with the elements are just that, traditional. If they don't seem to be lined up right for you, it's okay to change them around for your own personal use. Really, it's okay. The world won't end if you decide that winter reminds you more of Air because of the cold winds that sweep in from Canada, or if Water feels more appropriate in the East on your altar because you live on the Atlantic Ocean, or if Fire seems more logical in the north because you live south of the equator, or if Earth reminds you of dawn because of the warm scent of your morning garden. These associations were developed by cultures that live in a particular climate and era, and had particular cultural assumptions. For ourselves, we stick to the traditional placements when we do group magic, so that we all have something familiar to work with, and do whatever we want with regard to our own personal works.

Even the elements themselves can mix and match. For the crossing-points between them, we've developed this little chart:

1. *AIR*

Air of air is wind.

Fire of air is flammable gas.

Water of air is mist.

Earth of air is inert gas.

2. FIRE

Fire of fire is flame.

Water of fire is electricity.

Earth of fire is chemically created heat.

Air of fire is lightning.

3. WATER

Water of water is water.

Earth of water is ice.

Air of water is rain.

Fire of water is steam.

4. EARTH

Earth of earth is soil.

Air of earth is dust.

Fire of earth is lava.

Water of earth is sand.

And so on. You can create other associations yourself.

The next thing to consider in studying the magic of place is the next layer of spirit, which is non-elemental spirits. Every place has its "flavor"—while the city has a great spirit of its own, the smaller areas in it have their own energy as well, part subjects of and part fingers and toes of the larger city-soul. Large natural (and man-made) features such as trees, parks, ponds, lakes, reservoirs, graveyards, large statues or monuments, large old buildings that stand out, and so on, may all be carriers of local spirits. Look both at the places where people seem to gather in crowds to talk and meander and do leisurely business, and also places that people go only to be quiet and reverential without knowing why. These are probably telltale indications of local indwelling spirits. Make it your business to make at least a brief contact with them, if only to say hello—especially the ones that are in your neighborhood or that you will be passing regularly. If they know you, they can do small favors for you, such as shield you from prying eyes as you pass through their domain of influence, or help you look for someone or something you've lost in their area.

They will probably have different personalities. In Boston, a city that Raven lived in for five years, the local spirits seem to be clustered around the so-called "squares" (actually rarely square at all) such as Harvard Square, Central Square, Kenmore Square, Copley Square, and so on. The spirit that lives in cosmopolitan Harvard Square, with its tie-dyed street musicians and leather-jacketed kids lounging in the "Pit," is very different from Copley's indwelling spirit, which lives, Raven firmly believes, in the graceful statues of the Muses on the steps of the quiet and inviting public library. There may actually be rivalries or disagreements between adjacent local spirits—try to stay neutral, please. Local spirits, like the city-soul, can change with time as their architecture (bodies) and residents (sustenance) and general upkeep (health) changes. Yours will, too, as those things change for you.

The spirit of one area may be grouchy and loathe to help you with anything; we suggest doing some trash-gathering or planting some flowers in a public area or otherwise helping with maintenance if you want more cooperation. The spirit of another area may be more than willing to hear you, and you will feel strange sensations rushing through your body as it attempts to jabber furiously to you. Spirits often take up residence in buildings, although not necessarily residential ones. Perhaps living with humans full-time is too irritating for them, but we've noticed that they do tend to prefer public buildings that close down at night. Older ones are more likely to be inhabited than younger ones. Press yourself against the side of a building, as you would with a tree in the wild, and talk to the spirit. (You might want to make sure that no one is looking first, or if there's enough street people about muttering to themselves, perhaps it won't matter.)

You may want to make a spirit map of the city. Get hold of a street map, the bigger and more detailed the better, and decorate it with collage cutouts or other art. Each local spirit should be pictured on it, however you see them. Cover each area of the map with symbols of your impressions—perhaps that big elm tree with a face looking out, or that angel monument, or the grim spirit of the cemetery, the angry, fiery face of the combat zone—and hang it on your wall. It can be a work in progress, as you learn the city.

By learning the magical places in your city, you make it truly yours; the place where your feet are planted. If anything comes after you, it will be hitting you on your territory. When you need to do magic, you will be doing it from the home front, having the home team advantage, as it were, wherever you are. After a while you'll know instinctively where to go to bury that stone or salt-filled bottle, where to meditate, where to ask if your neighbor's cat has been seen around. It's worth it to talk to places. Not only do they talk back, but by touching them you touch forces that were created before you came and will be there long after you are gone, and add the memory of your touch to their subtle archives. And someday, some magician of a future generation may touch them, and touch that moment of you in turn.

eight

Fetishes

Junkyard Magic

• • The strength of an item of magic doesn't lie in its monetary value, or its beauty or age, or the fact that it was passed down from sorcerer to sorcerer. The wands, the knives, the incense and candles, these are all props. If they help your will to focus, or your mind to do the work, then they're worth all the trouble of acquiring, keeping, attuning, cleansing, and protecting them. However, if you're impoverished, desperate, or just out on a city street alone with no tools and the need to cast a fast spell, there are other things you can use as props, and they won't cost you a cent or be difficult to find.

Junkyard magic is the art of using discarded items of trash as the focus for your spells. The tiny bits of garbage that can be found scattered along the sidewalk or in empty lots can work for you if you put in the right effort and use your imagination. A spell made with such items will also have the additional bonus of being nearly unrecognizable to passersby. A small arrangement of crumpled gum wrappers, bits of broken glass, and an old cat food can won't be disturbed or even looked at twice, whereas a burning candle and a bunch of flowers might invite destruction from local idiots, albeit to their detriment.

If the gods want you to do a certain ritual or work of magic, they will provide the spell components for you; all you have to do is walk around with your eyes open and look for them. Many of us have had too much impregnation with *Dungeons & Dragons*-style fantasy, and we assume that ritual tools must be beautiful glass goblets or elaborate silver athames, that spell components must be patchouli incense and multiple-colored candles. If you have the funding for this (and the time to get it together), fine. If not—if you're impoverished or need a spell fast in a bad section of town—junk magic will work just as well, even if it's ugly or clumsy. It's the intent, channeled through the inanimate objects, that makes the difference.

Air Magic

We can start with the four elements, as many things in the average dumpster or junkyard have affinities with them. In the east, we have the direction of Air, of mind and thinking and speech. Broken glass is a good thing to associate with Air, which is related to knives and the suit of swords. This is because the mind cuts things apart, analyzes, slashes through them with sharpness. Broken glass can be clear, to indicate a wish for clarity of mind, or colored or cloudy, or even opaque. Use the non-clear varieties for warding spells that cloud or distract the minds of potential intruders. For either kind, arranging small pieces of broken glass in the shape of a letter, rune, or other symbol is the easiest way to handle it. Make sure that you touch them carefully; it's preferable to wear gloves. It's also perfectly all right to break them further if you need smaller pieces.

Another use for broken glass is as a quick ceremonial knife. One of the oldest tools known to man is a blade called a burin, which was usually chipped from a piece of volcanic glass. Broken bottle glass makes as good a burin as anything else might. Use it for engraving, cutting, or scraping objects such as bone, wood, plastic, or leather.

Any pieces of sharp metal also come under the heading of Air. This includes knives, bits of cut metal, and even tin can lids. (Again, take precautions when handling such things; we've sliced ourselves open on can lids more times than we can count.) One of the easiest magical items to make for talking to winds is a "wind chime" made of old can lids. Punch a hole in each one with a hammer and nail, and then string them up in rows with an inch or two of string between each one. Make two or three rows and hang them on a wire coat hanger, and hang it where the wind can get it and speak to you through it. This can be used for weather magic (asking the winds to bring you a certain kind of weather) or communication (asking them to carry a subliminal message to someone).

As mirrors are associated with Air and the mind, shiny pieces of tinfoil or old gum wrappers come under this heading as well. Use them for quickie mirror spells. These are usually cast on others in order to change their heads in a certain way, to make them see themselves and see the truth. You can wrap a symbol of that person in a gum wrapper, foil side in, and toss it. You can tuck it flat, foil side in, into the windshield wiper of their car, so they see it immediately upon sitting down in front of the steering wheel. You can fold it carefully into an arrow and leave it where they'll step over it, making a kind of psychic elf-shot. Remember that whenever you cast a spell on someone else, it bounces back on you. That's how you know it worked on them as well. So it's kind of like casting it on yourself too; keep this in mind.

Rolling up those silver wrappers into a ball indicates the moon, which is associated with mystery and the receptive nature. Leaving such an item where someone will come into contact with it will have the effect of getting them in touch with their inner selves—whether they like it or not.

Dropped bird feathers, such as pigeon feathers, are associated with Air (as is any place where birds gather) and have specifically to do with learning. Don't bring them with you; place them in a pattern where the wind can take them, and ask for the gift of the mind's flight. When you return a day later, if the wind has taken them, it means your gift has been granted.

Fire Magic

In the south, we have the powers of Fire, of energy and anger and passion and will. Fire can be represented by paper of any kind; paper burns easily, and it sounds like flame when it is crumpled. Paper folding, even of bits of trash, is a good way to do a surreptitious spell. Study origami if you like the idea; otherwise just practice folding small pieces of paper into specific shapes. They need not be extremely lifelike; in fact, if you want them to be overlooked, it might be better if only you can recognize the shape. Spells done by calling on the spirits of Fire will have dramatic and often unexpected and somewhat destructive results; if you ask for money, Fire may hit you with a car and break your leg, resulting—three years and innumerable physical therapy sessions later— in a financial settlement. Ask for love, and Fire will send you the girl or boy of your dreams . . . who's leaving town next month, never to return, and wants you to come with them. Fire is a life-changer.

To symbolize fire, take paper and crumple it in the middle so that the corners all stick up. This is a symbolic flame. High-proof alcohol—firewater—works as well, and you can douse your paper flame with a little of it, but make sure you aren't creating a real fire hazard if you walk off and leave it.

Cigarette butts and the contents of ashtrays are also good symbols of Fire. The old stubs are especially good for calming someone down or "putting out" their anger; relight the butt and put it out in a container of water, and then pour the resulting ashy water out onto the ground.

Many people smoke cigarettes. It's an unhealthy habit and it may kill you eventually, sacrificing you to the spirit of Fire, but some are unable to free themselves from its siren song. Cigarettes can be a useful magical item, if you aren't addicted to them. Those who have sacrificed themselves to the tobacco spirits, whose soul those spirits already own a piece of, cannot command or control these volatile devas. Those who don't normally smoke, however, can carry or use them to invoke Fire (or to bribe homeless street people to leave your car or motorcycle alone, or warn you if anything happens to them), or to pass as incense and thus invoke Air as well. You can draw runes in the air with the burning tip and they will stay on the aether for some time.

Those who carry cancer sticks also carry lighters or books of matches; these are also good Fire symbols to place on quick, impromptu altars. A lighter can also stand in for a magical torch; hold it overhead to drive off malicious influences.

Water Magic

In the west, we have the spirits of Water, of the feeling self, of emotions and compassion and love and sorrow. Water is symbolized by containers of any kind—cans, bottles, bottle caps, paper and Styrofoam cups, pots, pans, aluminum foil takeout dishes. There are many aesthetically pleasing ways to combine them for a spell; lay bottles in a triangle or starburst, stack cans in a castle shape. Facing up, where they can collect rain, they indicate receptivity; you're asking for a particular feeling or emotion to come into your heart, such as love or contentment or serenity. Facing down, they indicate a wish to be rid of an unwanted emotion, to let it run out onto the earth.

Clear glass bottles filled with a little water can be used to focus sunlight on a bright day to start ritual fires (be careful with this, however). The same bottle partially filled with water can be used as a glass harmonica and blown into for musical notes—don't overlook the magic of music. They can be used as a glockenspiel: just take a stick and ding different-sized ones, perhaps with different levels of water in them. They can also shelter candle flames from the wind, making impromptu sconces. The broken ones are good for this. Colored bottles give colored lights. With a twist of wick, floating on some oil, a glass bottle becomes an oil lamp. You can also float the last two or three matches in the matchbook as a wick. They can be filled with dark or light liquids and be used for scrying; bottle scrying has a long history in folk magic. The color of the glass may affect the "world" you look into.

One can make "cup markings," like one finds on ancient dolmens, using the mouth of a jar, some sand, and spit for lubricant. These mystical, rounded markings are found all over ancient monuments in the Celtic lands; they can symbolize the moon or sun, or the eyes of gods if made in pairs, or openings into the underworld. They can be made on any masonry surface: brick, stone, cement, concrete.

Of course, the classic bottle spell is always worth doing. For protection, fill it with nails, hawthorn spikes, sharp pieces of metal, and salt; place by your threshold, or bury it, if possible. If you want someone to look favorably on you, draw a picture of them, sweeten the lips with honey or whiskey, and then place it in the bottle and fill with flower petals and candy. For communing with spirits and entreating their help, fill it with weeds and small stones. For an offering to a deity, fill with his or her favorite items and bury it in a place they'd like. If you want to get rid of something, put its name in a bottle and toss it in a river or storm drain. Small liquor bottles work well for this, since they are unobtrusive and tend not to clog drains.

Plastic wrap also works well for Water, especially in a dry area where there's little likelihood of any rain coming and filling your containers. Stretch plastic wrap over the opening, or stuff it inside, wadded up. It can also be twisted into shapes that can represent certain strong feelings, and then smoothed out again.

Soap flake laundry detergent is another Water symbol, as it makes water foam like the sea. It is also an invisibility spell. If you think you're being followed by someone or something not exactly human, endeavor to pass by a laundromat. Duck inside and fish a couple of used containers of soap flakes out of the trash can. As you walk down the street, shake the last bits of soap flake out behind you, to magically "cover your tracks." Then turn a corner and don't look back; looking back will draw attention and ruin the spell.

Earth Magic

In the north, we have the Earth spirit: stability, strength, and acceptance of the body and the physical world. Earth is simple in terms of junk items: dirt, sand, dust, pebbles, weeds, twigs, chunks of cement or asphalt. The simplest spell utilizing these things is merely to take a stick and draw a figure in the dirt, symbolizing what you want. If it is something to be gained, leave it and walk away; if it is something to get rid of, scratch it out with your foot and then walk away. Don't look back.

The most common Earth spells have to do with money, and of course all coins are under the aegis of Earth. If you can't find an actual coin for a spell, even a penny, you can write an amount on a bottle cap and fill it with dirt and leave it on some high, flat surface where it will be undisturbed. However, coins can be difficult to enchant unless they are "faux" coins or really old ones that have been out of circulation for a long time. As a coin or dollar bill is passed from hand to hand, it picks up the energy of everyone it touches, and after months or years of this, it will be too cluttered to "take" a spell. However, old coin dealers have tons of old wheat pennies that sell for only about twice their original value, and fake bills are available in any joke shop. Monopoly money works well, too, if it hasn't been used all that often.

Flowers can be used for many spells involving peace and love. If you aren't lucky enough to have either flowering houseplants, a small yard with flowers, or permitted access to a neighbor's, the best place to acquire free flowers is the trash cans and dumpsters behind florists' shops. The spirits don't care if they're bruised or bedraggled.

These can be used as offerings for deities, or as spell components. One of the prettiest spells we've seen was a bunch of hippies making a huge peace sign out of trashpicked flowers in the middle of a public square, with a huge origami crane folded from a large piece of found cardboard in the middle. It lasted for about two hours, with passersby smiling and exclaiming rather than starting fights.

Scarecrow magic is the art of dressing up tree branches or posts in discarded clothing in order to create an urban golem. The suggestion of a presence can be created in dark alleys with branches, poles, or carpet cutouts dressed in human clothing, blessed, and left as guardians. Eyes can be made out of bottle caps, and hair out of carpet, old dead grasses, or tangled masses of recording tape. Phantom dogs, cats, and other animals can also be cut out of carpet remnants or flattened cardboard boxes. Old, discarded Sheetrock is good for this too. Such mannikins can be parked beside walls, leaned up against trees, or dangled with string from utility poles. The only limits are the imagination of the individual. The more complex care and effort that is devoted to the construction of such shadow people, the more effective they will be in performing their assigned task. Make sure to name them, and empower them with chanting and a smudge of incense, which can be as simple as a wave of a cigarette. Call them by their names whenever you see them.

> Golem, Golem, Golem,
> I made him out of clay,
> Put the name of God upon his tongue
> With Golem I shall play. . . .

Sung to the tune of "The Dreidl Song"

Spiderwebs can also be constructed out of unreeled recording tape, giving new purpose to old 8-tracks. These can have many magical uses: they can be vertical or horizontal, they can confuse, redirect, or deny access to an area. Pieces of broken glass can be dangled like dewdrops, or wind chimes hung from them to add a dimension of sound. The web can be used to "catch" negative energy or anger from passersby. Dental floss will also work for such things because of its extreme fineness and considerable strength. You can set a golem to watch it.

Children's dolls, broken or whole, are symbolic of urban "elves" —the urban version of the tomte or tontu. They can be placed in chorus lines or leaned up against walls as guardians or small golems. Their body parts can be used for healing spells to "stand in" for individuals who are not present.

Gumball machines, the kind with little prizes, are a wealth of materials for junk spells. You can do divination for the day by seeing what sort of thing comes out. You'll find whistles, little figures, and other interesting things, all of which can be used to symbolize something in a spell. Many of the items are contained in small spheres made of clear or partially clear plastic that pop apart; these are great containers for random spells. You can put pieces of rolled-up paper with requests, figurines, broken glass, rocks, plant bits, or whatever into them and bury them, or drop them down a sewer, or leave them in someone's yard under a bush, or toss them through an open window into the backseat of someone's car, or whatever.

A magical-use item that few people know about that is available in any gas station is the classic little tree-shaped car air freshener. As intimated in the movie *Repo Man*, these little tree air fresheners have more significance than just as scented cardboard. Their strong arrow-like shape and bold primary colors make them valuable assets for spells requiring strong action and/or direction. You can assign a different color and scent to each purpose. Green pine ones promote monetary increase; red cinnamon ones bring sex; vanilla is peace; and so forth. If you were to buy all of them, you could even use them as a divinatory "deck of cards," something even a visually impaired person could use, as they all have their own smell; they are durable and can be shuffled like playing cards.

The Romany use a particular kind of warding magic referred to as *baXt* (pronounced "bacht" with the guttural "ch"). This consists of a mixture of salt and hot spices, such as cayenne, ground chili peppers, black and white pepper, or paprika, which can be sprinkled on the ground as a protective boundary or tossed in the general direction of a potential psychic attack. It's pretty useful for physical attackers, too. An easy way to get a quick supply of baXt is to grab some salt and pepper packets from fast-food restaurants. Likewise, pepper spray wards off magical attacks as well as physical ones.

To claim an area as being magically safe for your family, create a heraldic coat of arms (if you don't already have one) and make a heraldic tableau with junk in a nearby alley. You might use pieces of colored cardboard boxes for background, a doll's arm holding a tinfoil weapon, origami heraldic beasts, and the like.

Stones are quintessentially earth—but in junk magic, it isn't the type of stone you use so much as what you do with it. Stones can be piled on each other, even in small pebble pyramids, or laid in a circle, or given as offerings. If you observe an interesting stone on the street, pick it up and examine it very carefully. Try to read the stone like you would read tea leaves in the bottom of a cup. Look for interesting crystal inclusions, cracks, fissures, or faults. Consider what message this particular stone that you've picked up has for you at this particular place and time. When you've absorbed the lesson, put the stone back so that it can instruct someone else.

Certain stones are particularly good for being made into burins, or ceremonial knives. The silicate stones (flint, agate, chert, and obsidian) split conchoidally, which means that when you knock off a flake with a harder rock, it looks like a tiny scallop shell. Flaking a blade carefully can result in a knife that is sharper than steel, and is a link to the way our ancestors lived. Rough chipping is done with a round stone, called a hammerstone, with a dense rock like granite or quartzite. "Finish" (shaping) chipping can be done with a pressure-flaking method, which used to be done with an antler; use a hardwood stick or piece of bone. Place the knife on your leg, wrapped in a piece of leather, and apply the tip to where you want to break off the edge, and apply the wooden pick with a twisting motion, so as to snap off a shell-shaped piece of stone. This takes a good deal of practice, but the same techniques can be used with common bottle glass. They can be hafted (in an old soup bone if you like) as a knife, bringing the flavor of the Neolithic age to the canyons and rock shelters of the modern urban environment.

The majority of city surfaces—brick, cement, concrete, asphalt—all lend themselves well to being marked on with a stone, can, or other sharp object. In this way, you can lay down runes and other symbols for a warding or message spell.

Graffiti is a magical thing. It can be placed as wards or other spells, and already-existing graffiti can be utilized as well, even if their creators had no intention of magic. Any or all naked women or female body parts, no matter how badly drawn, are figures of the Goddess and thus can be invoked for her protection. Consider it to be a work of reclaiming. Decorated words can be interpreted and used as backgrounds for altars or as part of a warding spell.

You can do junk divination as well. When you leave your home in the morning, take note of what you come across as you go, and it will give you a clue to what your day may hold. A coin may presage money, a paper gum wrapper may intimate something difficult to chew on, or an empty Styrofoam cup, on its side, may indicate the need to let go of some emotion that refuses to wear away and is harmful to your existence. Use your intuition to decide what the meaning might be; let the object suggest its own meaning to you.

More advanced urban shamans may wish to attempt construction of a wizard-walk maze or labyrinth. This requires a strong knowledge of your city, and preferably a map of it. Trace out a maze on the map; it can be a classic eight-turn labyrinth (which you should learn to make from other books or teachers) or a random maze. Then walk it, from its starting point to its end, and line it with unobtrusive sigils, signs, spells, altars, webs, and so on. It should be constructed so that someone who has no knowledge of urban magic won't notice enough to follow it.

Mazes can be used to disappear into or, more commonly, as a way to walk between worlds, to create a safe portal to move from one reality to another. The final point of the maze should be a place one can be fairly certain of being undisturbed, or it can wind around on itself and send you back out to the starting point, except that now you're on a slightly different plane of reality and can see the unseen. Of course, that means that the unseen can now see you as well, and you should be careful when passing back through the maze that they don't follow you. This can be accomplished by sprinkling various substances behind you as you go—soap flakes for invisibility, tangled wires for traps of confusion, salt for neutralization, baXt spices for a barrier.

nine

Travois

VEHICLE CHARMS

• • Raven took a course in basic mechanics once, given by a local garage. The teacher, in crisp red coveralls, spoke in an exasperated tone about how people foolishly imbue their cars with supposed intelligence and sentience, referring to them as "him" or "her" and pretending that they were living creatures with needs and desires. This, the mechanic continued, was foolish because sooner or later they would break down and then the owners would feel betrayed and berate what was, after all, only a big chunk of metal with a lot of moving parts.

He decided not to mention the time that his big 1972 Dodge van, Lurch, had of his own accord (and in spite of his frightened wife's efforts) changed lanes to avoid an oncoming speeder. It would only have caused trouble, and anyway the mechanic wouldn't have believed it. Maybe it's true. Maybe cars are just big hunks of metal with no indwelling soul. But we doubt it. We've driven cars with all sorts of personalities, and we have noticed that the more you drive them, the more they respond like a steed rather than a machine. If we can transfer energy to a stone or wand, we can transfer it to a car.

Energies for Your Vehicle

car dragons

When Raven first learned to drive, a friend taught him about car dragons. These were ethereal spirits, she explained, that could be invoked to take up residence in your vehicle. They would watch out for oncoming trouble and warn you if it was coming, remind you when the gas and oil were low, camouflage you from the police, and could even, in some cases, keep you from getting lost. They communicate by hunches and mental pictures. The problem with car dragons is that if you don't take excellent care of the car, getting repairs quickly when needed, they can become offended and leave. Theoretically, a car dragon can be switched over to your next car when the last one dies, but it's better to dismiss it and invoke another, as different kinds of cars attract different kinds of dragons.

To invoke a car dragon, you tuck sticks of burning incense into the front bumper and go for a drive, preferably somewhere quiet and private, like a big grocery store parking lot at midnight. As you drive around in circles, request a car dragon to take up residence. Seduce it by telling it all the wonderful places you'll go, and how it will always have your companionship, at least until the car croaks. Picture it floating down and settling onto the roof of the car, and ask its name. It may not tell you. Dragons are like that.

Then it's up to you to keep it in state. A car dragon may require a lot of upkeep, and perhaps you should only invoke one if you think you're going to be able to afford prompt repairs. Another option is to let the car develop its own indwelling spirit, which takes time and a lot of driving about. An old car that has passed through many hands will probably already have its own spirit, although some say that major trauma, such as engine replacement or rebuilding from a wreck or even being abandoned by its' people, will cause the spirit to flee, and you'd have to start over.

altars

Whatever the case, the first thing you should do is to create an altar for your car. Find a small Matchbox-style car that resembles yours; paint it the right color and add any racing stripes or other markings that it may have. Set it on a shelf somewhere on black paper with a white dotted line down the middle, surrounded by a bunch of small plastic bottles or tightly capped containers containing offerings of the five elemental car fluids. Place transmission fluid slightly to the east of the car, gasoline in the south, antifreeze to the west, brake fluid to the north, and motor oil in the center. Add a few coins or bills of Monopoly money to represent there always being enough cash to fix the car if necessary, including a highway token. Add a piece of a map to keep from getting lost, a pair of fuzzy dice to keep you safe on the road, and maybe add a "little tree" air freshener for good measure.

Note: The above fluids are somewhat dangerous to keep in your house, especially around children and pets. Gasoline especially is flammable, and antifreeze is poisonous and smells edible to pets. Make sure that the containers these fluids are kept in are unbreakable and well sealed, so that if they get knocked off they absolutely will not spill. If you are not comfortable with keeping these fluids on the altar at all, an alternative is to use the labels off the product bottles, or cards inscribed with the molecular structure of the fluids. When you want to dismantle the altar, please dispose of the fluids properly at a recycling center. Don't just dump them. Your city is polluted enough.

fetishes

The next item is creating a fetish. Most times the fetish is hung off of the rear-view mirror, although if it gets too large and unwieldy you may want to put it elsewhere. Just make sure that it doesn't block your view. Some people have specific items that they hang; others add to it continuously as they find interesting things, perhaps stuff they pick up on the road. One of our best protective fetishes, the one that kept Raven's decrepit 1972 Dodge van going for more than a decade, consisted of a shark's jaw (for protection), a Kali's belt of severed Barbie doll heads (for even more protection in Boston traffic), a pair of small scissors (for cutting through bureaucratic red tape), a gold necklace (for cash needed in order to drive), a stuffed toy crow (for vigilance), and a toy wrench (for honest mechanics). Raven also added occasional pendants or stones from places he'd stopped on road trips, as a form of appreciation that Lurch (the name for the van) had gotten him there safe and sound.

sticky things

Chinese boatmen paint eyes on the prow of their boats so that they may see oncoming vessels and be more agile in taking evasive action. You can do this for your car, too. There are plenty of stickers out there shaped like eyes. Place them in the center or upper corners of the windshield. Smaller is better, so as not to block the driver's vision. If you can't find any, you can make them out of cut-down bumper stickers or contact paper.

Bumper stickers themselves are a great source of car magic. These days, most bumper stickers are political in nature, expressing people's heartfelt opinions. Most of the folks who avoid bumper stickers do so for this reason—they don't want their opinions publicly known. But nothing says that a bumper sticker has to be political, or even have words on it. It can have a single symbol, or a pretty design, something inoffensive that no one will be bothered by. It can still have an effect on them, though. Remember that your back bumper and rear windshield are the parts of your car that will be the most scrutinized by other drivers. Perhaps you might choose a design that is enspelled to be calming and peaceful, so that the irritability of the driver behind you might not escalate, or perhaps a warding-off design to prevent rear-ending. Similar warding-off stickers might be discreetly placed on the side doors to prevent sideswiping, and on the front bumper to prevent head-on collisions. We find yin-yang symbols to be good peace-inducing designs, and we use the bind rune Othila, the shield, as a warding-off sign.

Almost any print shop can make you a specialized bumper sticker, and contact paper in interesting designs works in a pinch, although it has a tendency to peel off after some weathering. Even small stickers can work. Stick-on reflectors—called "hot dots" in some areas—can be massed to form a design.

not just for cars

All these tricks can be utilized for non-automobile forms of vehicle as well. Not everyone has a car; many city dwellers resort to bicycles or even skateboards, and some own motorcycles or mopeds. The magical difference between two-wheeled and four-wheeled vehicles, however, is mostly one of perception. Rather than a dragon or other large monster, bikes of all types are generally seen as steeds. Raven's wife actually had a favorite bicycle that she referred to as "Pony," and many motorcycle riders secretly or openly think of their machines as metal horses of some kind. Riding a bike is recapturing some of the horseback travel of old times—you sit astride, open to the weather and feeling the road.

In medieval times, knights often treated their horses better than they treated their wives. Horses were coddled—until the battlefield, when they might die en masse. At any rate, the bike is psychically closer to the palfrey, the pleasure riding horse, than to the destrier, or warhorse. It's not inappropriate to name your bike as if it were a steed, and invoke a "spirit horse" into it. All the car magic, from altars to stickers, works for bikes as well, motorized or otherwise. There's also the added side benefit of the helmet, which is a nice flat space to put protective runes on, especially ones to keep your head from getting split open. For bicycles, making your symbols in reflective paint or stickers is especially good. Raven's wife covered her bike helmet in runes made with glow-in-the-dark paint, which is available in craft stores. This is not only safer for the nighttime rider, it also allows the symbols to absorb the light of the sun or the moon and thus add their magic and power to the spell. (The magical properties of glow-in-the-dark paint are, in general, badly underestimated. Making symbols on cars, walls, or other items that are unobtrusive until the lights go down is a fine way to work a spell.)

The Spirit of the Road

If you do a lot of car travel or long road trips, you may want to do magic to propitiate the spirit of the road. Some people like to talk to deities that have been traditionally assigned traveling as their bailiwick; Ellegua and Hermes/Mercury come to mind. Raven prefers to go straight to the spirit of the road, which is what he calls that nameless force who rules the ever-moving lands, whose arteries are highways and whose capillaries are back roads and whose heart is never found, but always sought. He invokes the spirit of the road either by singing while he drives or by making maps in the dirt by the side of the road with a stick. It seems to like that. Since he is spatially dyslexic and it's very easy for him to get lost, the most frequent thing that he calls upon the spirit of the road for is finding his way. As he draws the little play-map in the dirt at the side of the road, asking the spirit for its help, sometimes the right way to go will pop right into his head.

Offerings to the spirit of the road should be released out the vehicle window while the vehicle is moving, preferably at high speed.

Don't think that offering it empty beer cans and McDonalds burger wrappers is a cute idea. It is definitely offended by litter. Stick to natural, biodegradable materials such as a feather, a flower, a piece of food or dribble of drink, or a bit of dried herb. Remember that whenever you are on the road, you are under the protection of the spirit of the road. You can ask it for directions, for safety, or even for help should you stall out on a lonely roadway—it can find help and send it along. If you hitchhike—a dangerous hobby that we do not recommend, but some people do it—we strongly suggest that you dedicate yourself formally to the spirit of the road and ask its protection as a permanent order, so that you don't end up dead in a ditch somewhere. We're not sure what it will ask of you in return, but we're sure that it will be interesting.

Spirit of the Road

I call you with the morning sun and the evening's purple glow,
It's time again to go.
I echo through the pine trees and the mountain's high retreat,
And the city streets,
Low and sweet,
I lie along the land like a ribbon in the curve of a lover's hair,
Come and share.
I'm the song of your greatest longing and the world that you've
  yet to see,
Come follow me,
Come and be free . . .

My music drags you out the door and far away to roam,
I take you to adventure and I bring you safe back home,
I'm the song of the wind and the wheels on the pavement
And I lighten your heavy load,
But don't mind me, I'm just the Spirit of the Road . . .

Raven Kaldera, 1990

ten

Sustenance

Job Finding and Keeping

• • When it comes to professional magic—people asking witches and magicians to do spells for them—the number-one request, bar none, is for money and job spells. Unless you're lucky enough to have the perfect job, from which you'll never be fired and with which you'll never get bored, you'll probably end up pounding the pavement at some point during your life.

However, once you've found the perfect job—or at least something that will pay the bills and that you don't despise too much—you have to be able to keep it. Part of that task is yours; all the magic in the world won't help you if you continually show up late or skip work, don't do assigned tasks, cut corners, and so on, but sometimes things may happen that are beyond your control. Maybe the company has a financial dip and needs to lay off some workers. Maybe troublesome coworkers are trying to get you fired. Maybe your boss doesn't like something about you that is beyond your control, such as your gender, sexual preference, race, or religion. These are the issues that can be addressed with magic.

As always, magic that is directly aimed at another specific human being has to be handled very carefully, because it will also be cast on you, whether you like it or not. Whenever possible, avoid it. For example, rather than putting a spell on the boss, just do a spell against firing in general. If you must put a spell on someone, don't attempt to lay anything on them that you wouldn't gladly accept for yourself. If you think that the boss needs a change of perspective and you put him in a mirror spell, resign yourself to the fact that you, too, will be facing some difficult truths that you didn't know you were in denial about, very soon. If you do a binding spell on someone to prevent them from engaging in what you perceive as unfair behavior, be aware that you probably have some unfair behaviors yourself, and you will suddenly find yourself unable to engage in them, which may feel pretty uncomfortable. Every spell cast on another person should also be seen as an opportunity for cathartic and possibly painful self-improvement. If you're afraid of that, keep your spells general rather than personal.

Getting a job

There are two different magics involved in getting jobs and keeping them. The first step is becoming gainfully employed. To get jobs, use a red candle for Mars energy, which is aggressive, assertive, and active. This is especially important when there is competition involved for the position. Use a red novena candle, and paint or tape three symbols on it. First, paint on it a symbol of either the job itself, or just income (dollar sign) if you don't care about what sort of job it is. Use a business card from the company you wish to employ you, or a clipping from the newspaper that notifies of job openings there, or just a drawn symbol of the type of employment, such as a cash register, or desk, or truck. Then paint or tape the symbol for aid on it. Tacky as it sounds, we use a little red cross on a white background with little blue wings. Then paint or tape the sign of Mars—the circle with the arrow pointing out at an angle (♂)—so that the circle encompasses the aid symbol and the arrow points right to the job. (If the energy doesn't know where to go after that, it's hopeless and you might as well hang it up.) Anoint the candle with mint oil for money and cinnamon oil for energy; mint tea and sprinkled cinnamon will do if you don't have any oils. Take a net and wrap it around the base of the candle to "capture" your job. If you don't have a piece of netting, one of those plastic net bags for onions from the supermarket will work fine.

Don't light your candle just yet. Get in the car, or on a bus or train, and go downtown to city hall. Stand in front of it and have a conversation with the spirit of the city, and the spirits of all the dead city founders. Say how much you like living here in this city, and explain that if you are to stay, you are going to need a job to put a roof over your head and food in your belly. If you have children or other dependents, mention them. Ask for help and specify the type of work. State where you live, and explain if the work needs to be in walking or biking distance from you—important if you have no car. These guys are under no obligation to help you out, so make it convincing. Leave an offering of food or drink or pennies, thank them, and go home. Light your candle and visualize the job you want.

Another good spell uses magnets. Any magnet will do, even a fridge magnet. In fact, you can stick a picture of you onto the fridge magnet, and then use it to trap the business card or newspaper clipping to the fridge while you go for the interview. For interviews themselves, carry a magnet on you, or three shiny pennies tied in a green cloth (make them shiny by soaking them in vinegar), or wear High John the Conqueror Root oil or dragon's blood oil, or, if you can find one, a pin shaped like a horseshoe, worn points-up to capture the luck.

If your job has a particular sort of patron, make an offering to them as well. For example, a child-care position or social worker would be the province of the Mother Goddess in her most nurturing form. A skilled machinist or hardware position might be Hephaestus, a construction job Ptah, a phone or traveling job Mercury, and so forth We suggest invoking Athena for any job requiring precision office work or research, or for the "high corporate" world in general. Remember that she prefers her charges to be heroes, so you'd better be prepared to be one.

Some people swear by spells that make them look like a VIP: invoking Jupiter, wearing purple, lighting a purple candle with their name taped to it, visualizing the interviewer seeing them as a special person. This can work great or backfire, depending on the particular interviewer. You may be turned down for seeming too self-important, or too overqualified. Be sure you know the venue well first.

One reason that people may have difficulty getting and keeping jobs is lack of the kind of team-player, persona-mask social skills that grease workplace relations. They may lack the ability to assume the proper attitude at will. For instance, if you have problems with authority and can't keep a job because of it, try making an offering to Tammuz/Dumuzi/Ing, the Corn King who willingly submits to a higher authority in order to support a greater good (bread and beer are a good offering). If you don't work well with others, make an offering of something sweet to the Love Goddess in order to sweeten your attitude. If you always say the wrong thing, ask Hermes/Mercury to make your tongue more glib.

Keeping a job

Now that you've got the job, the next thing is to keep it. First, guard against layoffs. Take a slip of pink paper, write LAID OFF on it in big letters, roll it up, and stick it in the very back of your freezer. Make sure that one of your kids or housemates doesn't accidentally pull it out while searching for Popsicles, as the spell could be damaged or disrupted.

The color used for keeping a job is green. Get a green candle and stick the business card of your company on it, and anoint the wick with mint oil. Light it, say, "I belong here," and then put out the flame. Repeat the spell about once every week.

You can also make a mojo bag of herbs associated with money and business: fennel seed, sesame seed, flax seed, fenugreek, or mint, with some shiny coins and a rock or two for steadfastness. I usually add some play money and a smiling face for raises and pleased bosses. Don't add personal items such as underwear or hair clippings—you may actually want to leave this company someday, if things go sour. Then secrete the bag somewhere on the premises of the company. Don't put it in your office. Put it as close as possible to the headquarters of the company. Burying it in the dirt at the base of the ubiquitous potted plant works well. Should you decide to quit, retrieve the bag. If it's nowhere to be found, take this as a sign that you should leave. Now.

If you're actually a small business owner yourself, or partner in a business, you'll be doing the magic not to get or keep your job, but to get or keep your company going. The VIP spell that is iffy in job interviews works really well when trying to impress bank reps who could lend you money. Keep your green candle going, as in the above-mentioned spell, but instead of saying "I belong here," say, "We are strong and solid and we float."

Sometimes the threat is more than financial. A local witch shop owner had some neighborhood issues over her store for a while. A friend came back from the local CrimeWatch meeting, reporting that some neighbors were worried that because the store sold incense, it also might be selling drugs. The allegations were supposedly largely the work of a campaigning local politician. Afterwards, she got a surprise visit from a city inspector. She put together a spell to ward off any potential neighbor and civic difficulties by lighting a red candle (for Mars), anointed with patchouli (for a musky marking of your territory), vetivert (for earthy solidity), cinnamon (for Mars), and fenugreek (for financial continuation). She attached a simple clip-art picture of a dragon (for strength), and the phrase "Protect the Nest," and burned it for seven days until it was gone. The result was that a friendly advisor came into her life and helped her satisfy the city inspectors, and other neighborhood business owners stood up for her in the CrimeWatch meeting and embarrassed the harassers into dropping the subject. The politician, just as an aside, suffered an embarrassing defeat. This sort of spell is useful for any small business, but businesses that are unusual or counterculture need extra protection.

eleven

Tribal Markings

Clothing and Body Decoration

• • The first part of this chapter, on clothing, is written by Raven, and the second part, on body modification, is by Tannin, since these are our personal specialties. In each segment, we use the first-person "I" pronoun to describe our experiences.

Part I: Wearable Spells

I'm a magical costumer, and I do it for a living. People come to me and ask me to re-create them into the images of their fantasies, whether that might be a dominatrix in leather corseting, an alien wandering around a science-fiction convention, or maybe just the most beautiful wedding dress in the world. It's a kind of sacred theater, and it can have far-reaching repercussions.

I started out doing Halloween costumes for myself and my friends, and then progressed to theater companies. It was when I started to actively create special costumes for magical work that things began to get weird, however; once started, it refused to stop. The energy spilled over until every piece that I made began to have strange effects for people, even when they'd only ordered a simple Halloween costume. The wearer of the Earth Mother outfit suddenly became pregnant, even after being told it was impossible; the individual who went to a mythical-creature theme party dressed in my phoenix costume leaned over a candle and went up in flames. As I looked back on my last few Samhain costumes, I realized that they had each set the tone for the succeeding year—and I began to take it all far more seriously.

Costume magic—and its predecessor, mask magic—is shape-shifter magic. You take on the appearance of something or someone else, and you absorb its energy. Your choice of clothing and accoutrements can invite or repel a deity or spirit, grant or prevent a feeling, create or defend against an opportunity. This is far more than just the simple wearing-something-you-like-makes-you-feel-good sort of situation—if it's done ritually, in a ceremonial state of mind, it becomes an act of magic that does not depend on your mood or responses. In fact, it may take over and affect those responses quite strongly.

We've all heard about ways to use clothing, such as wearing a certain color for a certain effect, although I've found that the uses of different colors are really quite subjective—for one person blue is serenity, for another conformity; for one individual red is courage, and for another it's anger. We've also all probably either used or at least run into the idea of the lucky hat, the special shirt, or the winning jacket or tie that gains magical energy due to its repeated association with success. We can be much more conscious about clothing and its magical uses, though; each garment we put on can have a use if we decide to will it so.

In a sense, all clothing is costume; every "look" is a performance. We perform our gender, our class, our ethnic group, religion, goals, and sexual availability every day. We have our work costume, which is created by the needs of our job; mine is heavy boots and tough pants and flannel shirts, as I work at an outside job, and my corporate friends wear very different clothing. Often, it defines us; we act differently when wearing our work face. Then there's our "fun" costume, which we would wear for a night out; it might vary from simply and comfortably casual to explicitly sexual, depending on where we spend our nights out and what we hope to achieve there. Formalwear is an "impress me" costume. Even the clothes that we change into when we don't expect to be seeing anyone can be considered a "privacy" costume.

As a personal exercise, make some lists. The first should be a list of colors. Decide for yourself what each one implies when worn. Then make a list of the most worn items in your wardrobe, and write down what you think each of them suggests to others when you wear them. Then cross-check your lists with people. Ask your friends to make their own color lists, and then compare them. There may be glaring differences; that's okay. Compare how, for example, the color red comes across to each person. Do all the responses fall into one general category, or are they all different? Then ask your friends what they think of your list of garments, when you're wearing them. Do they all agree that you come across as cool in that leather jacket, or do some of them class it as pretentious?

What, you may ask, has this got to do with magic? Well, it brings home the two uses that costume magic is generally created for. One is for personal self-creation—for example, wearing that lucky shirt to give yourself courage and good fortune—and the other is to make a particular impression on other people.

Type A is easy. All you have to think about is your own lists. If that tie makes you feel strong or spiffy, great. If you want to applique a big mandala on the back of your vest in order to keep away evil spirits, terrific. Nobody else's opinion matters.

Type B isn't easy at all. Here, what you're trying to do is to influence other people's perceptions of you, and that's notoriously difficult.

That's the point of those lists that you have your friends make—to show you just how difficult it is. If red means strength and courage to you, and you wear your favorite red scarf to the job interview, and the person interviewing you has strong feelings that red is too flashy and indicates an impulsive, temperamental nature, there's a clash about to happen. Even if you deliberately ensorcelled that red tie, waving incense about it and commanding it to act as an indicator of your will and bravery to those who might view it, if your spell is going up against someone else's deeply ingrained, semiconscious prejudices . . . well, maybe it'll prevail and maybe it won't.

In medieval times, this magical talent was referred to as *glamour*—as in "the fairies cast a glamour over those dried leaves to make them appear to be gold coins," and so forth. Unlike its modern usage, the old meaning of glamour was to magically enchant something to make it appear different (usually better) than it actually was. It's the lightest and most noninvasive level of shapechanging magic: the ability to cast an illusion on yourself. Enchanting clothing and accessories is the time-honored way to accomplish this, and for good reason.

A first suggestion is to cut down on the amount of fighting internal prejudice you'll have to do. Although it is theoretically possible to go to a job interview stark naked except for a pink tutu and still get the job, the amount of magic you'd have to put out in order to compensate is hardly worth it. But how, you question, can I possibly know what the subconscious associations of people I've never met could be? Ask, I say. A good way to divine color or clothing choices for a particular situation is to create a bunch of clothing cards. They can be as simple as index cards with fabric pasted on them in various colors, or perhaps your outfits drawn on them. Treat them like a Tarot deck; ask them, "What will work best to achieve my goals today?" and pull a card.

(Of course, like any Tarot deck or other forms of divination, the color/clothing cards can sometimes second-guess you in ways you don't expect. For example, if wearing a red dress to that sports bar is highly likely to get you noticed by that serial killer, the cards may suggest a dowdier outfit that gets you home lonely and disgusted but still alive. If the job you're applying for is one you'll hate, they might recommend the suit that the interviewer will turn his nose up at. It's hard to tell, and there's a lot you might have to take on faith.)

Then, once the outfit is chosen, you can do what it takes to make it into a spell component. You can lay it on or hang it over your altar for a time. You can wave incense around it, assuming that the scent won't be a problem for whatever purpose it is to serve. You can embroider a symbol on an inside hem, or stitch in a crystal or small stone. You can sew or paint something on the inside neck tag of a shirt or dress. If it's a party outfit, you don't have to be discreet—spangles or studs can make a design in full view.

Jewelry is in a category all its own. It can be made, if you're crafty, and almost anyone can make a pendant out of Fimo or string some beads. Jewelry actually tends to hold magic even better than fabric, perhaps because it's more solid, so be especially careful and don't forget what's been laid on them. I once ensorcelled a ring to be a kind of invisibility spell, allowing me to pass unnoticed, and then absently wore it to a party where I became offended because no one was speaking to me.

I've heard it said that washing ritual or magical garments takes all the energy out of them and you have to start all over. Bosh, say I. The washing is only purificatory if you need it to be so. What will lose you the energy is leaving something around in a back drawer for a long time without touching it. The more you use something for its purpose after the enchantment, the stronger it'll get. The more you ignore it, the less it'll have. Even if you're not going to use it very often, periodically taking it out and touching it, concentrating on its power, will do the trick. Much of magic has to do with the right kind of attention paid to your energized items.

Just as it's important to pay attention to your magic clothing, it's also important to give them a rest. As I said, glamour is the lightest form of shapechanging magic. It doesn't actually change you in a deep way, it just lays a mask over your face. However, if you wear a magical mask too long, it can get stuck to you. It's a long, slow process and it can sneak up before you know it; one day it's just a mask and the item of clothing is just a tool, and the next day it's who you are, and you can't bear to lose that piece of cloth or leather or jewelry. The shapechanging magic went deeper, and changed your actual shape. If that's what you intended, great; if not, you may need to do a ritual to magically free yourself of your own spell. Be careful to think through what you do before you do it.

Some "everyday" forms of costume are more than just your personal fantasy. They tap into the cultural subconscious, and when you put them on you're putting on a collective mask whose meaning has been agreed upon on some level by everyone in our culture. This gives you extra power, the power of many generations of strong meaning, but it also traps you into a certain stereotype in other people's eyes. Since it's coming from the collective unconscious, they may not even be consciously aware of why they're treating you this way when you're dressed like that. What follows is some of the most obvious of these archetypal costumes, the ones that you're likely to meet on the street or be wearing yourself.

white knights—going into battle

A pagan friend called me to talk about the "corporate uniform," and as someone who has shunned corporate America since I was fired from my first desk job at the age of eighteen, I was surprised to hear his thoughts. "Isn't the uniform, well, exactly what it says, a uniform?" I asked. "Boring, restrictive of creativity, cog in the machinery, and all that?"

"There is a military slant to it," he said, "because the corporate world is a battlefield. No matter how user-friendly we try to make it, it's still a battlefield to the extent that there is capitalism, which involves brutal competition. There are battles, and casualties, and all the rest. So we really are soldiers going into battle. But if you look at records and pictures of the military hundreds of years ago, you'll see that they didn't all wear identical cookie-cutter uniforms. That came along with the industrial-era thinking, and the ability to provide identical clothing. Today's corporate world isn't based on an industrial model; they may lead industry, but they're more like the feudal lords of old.

"There was a great deal of creativity and pride in uniforms of that era, when they could afford it. Look at the companies of German Landsknecht in the sixteenth century! Slashes and ribbons and puffs and all of them different. There was a certain utility to it all, for the sake of practicality, but it helped morale to have that kind of peacocking. So, for example, don't think of your tie as just a piece of fabric that hangs over your shirt buttons. Your tie is a banner, a pennon, a flag to carry into battle. As such, it can be enspelled to help you bring victory. Choose colors and subtle patterns that convey, in your mind, the virtues of strength, endurance, and vision, or anything else you think might help. Use it like a magical item. I mean, they call them 'power ties' for a reason! Similarly, when you put on that suit, imagine it as armor, that you're about to go into battle and be victorious.

"If you don't like to think of yourself as a warrior, think of yourself as warrior support. Armies traveled with huge cavalcades in feudal days—often more cooks, employees, families of the soldiers, and so forth, than there were actual fighters. Without their support train, they'd never make it."

This is the same individual who encouraged me to think of lawyers as champion duelists, in the same way that if you were challenged to a duel in the old days and you were a weakling, you hired a champion to do it for you; the idea being that there's no shame in being or hiring a professional duelist to get you out of unwanted trouble.

black knights—the skins of our brothers

Leather, especially black leather, is and has always been terribly popular in our culture as a statement of strength, of toughness, of in-your-face outcastness. Leather shines with connotations of power, but why? There is the fact that it is the skins of animals sacrificed for our pleasure . . . we are wearing death, in our own way, personifying Skuld the Fate and the many other sacred deities of death and change. Leather has also been referred to as organic armor—armor that protects and yet still breathes, strong but still supple, unlike immutable metal.

Leather is skin—second skin. The first real clothing may well have been the skins of animals; certainly every one of those early ancestors knew the story behind every pelt that they wore. Each had been acquired at a cost, and not only their risk of life and limb. In order that they might survive and be protected, the life of an animal brother or sister had to be sacrificed. Even when we learned how to weave vegetable fibers into cloth, certain occupations—hunters, warriors, and shamans—still wore skins. In the case of the hunters, the pelts were both bragging rights and a way to honor the spirit of the brother who had died for them. The warriors often wore the skins of strong or predatory animals in order to confer upon themselves the courage of these furred kin, and to take advantage of leather's physically sturdy and protective qualities. Shamans wore the skins as fetishes, to commune with their totem creatures.

Today's leather garments generally come from domestic animals, and are slaughtered rather than hunted, but when we wear hide, we are forming a link with our ancestors, and some part of us knows it and is drawn to it. Our warrior energy is clothed in organic armor, drawn from living bodies, so that we might take its life force to protect our own. Brown leather echoes the hunter's path—stealth, blending into the landscape, passing unnoticed. Brightly colored leather is sensuous, calls attention, shows off our carnal natures, advertises our sexuality.

Black leather, the most popular color for armor, is indicative of the archetype of the Black Knight. When you put it on, you take on his archetype as well. What can we learn from this shadowy figure, sometimes called the Dark Rider, or the Dark Horse?

Unlike the White Knight, who is the champion who stands for your country, your society, whatever it is that is familiar to you and whose rules you understand and approve of, the Black Knight is the archetype of the Adversary. Although many Black Knights are guardians, standing in the road and protecting an entryway, others are wanderers, flying from place to place on the back of the wind. One is reminded of the obscure Norse deity Valraven, king and consort of the Underworld Goddess Hel, whose job was to be guardian and guide into the Land of the Dead, but who was also associated with the winged black horse, which was his shapeshifted form. When he rode the skies in this form, Valkyries rode on his back to collect the souls of dead heroes.

The Black Knight is Antihero, but not Villain. His figure also implies a code of honor, but possibly one that is different from your own—you are not completely certain that he will fight "fair" by your rules. He may have his own agenda, and it may be about getting in your face and preventing you from doing something. What he does, he does not because it is "right," but because it is what he personally feels is appropriate. He can be an avatar of chaos, a highwayman who assaults you for selfish reasons, a warrior gone bad; or he can be the outcast with honor, who exists to challenge your perceptions and widen your worldview. The line is thin between the two, and those who take on this mask often cross back and forth over it, if they are lacking in willpower and ethics.

What the Black Knight archetype seems to remind most people of is the moment when he steps across your path and challenges you to a duel in order to go on your way, and that's how people will instinctively react to you on first glance. Whether they end up seeing you as Mad Max or Darth Vader will depend on how you handle the situation, on whether or not your honor shows. Those of us who wear black leather need to understand this myth, and how we tap into it every time, regardless of our desires. Sometimes myths are powerful enough that they come and get you, and you can go willingly or kicking and screaming. It is always better to be conscious about it—to formally agree to wear the archetype well, or else formally take off the skin mask and reject it.

t-shirts: flying the flags of art

Another peculiarly modern piece of clothing that can work as a magic spell is the T-shirt. Not since the days of heraldry, when people wore their family and liege arms embroidered or painted on everything they owned, has there been such an explosion of clothing bearing complex symbols that are meant to be seen. T-shirts are both art and advertising, humor and attention-getting. When you put one on, remember that it's not just about what people will see and read. In a sense, a T-shirt's art affects your own aura, especially if it's one you wear again and again.

I had one particularly black-humor T-shirt that featured a scruffy man attempting to blow his brains out with a gun, and then commenting with disgust on how he'd missed. I was depressed at the time, and after a while noticed how, on my worst days, I'd reach for that T-shirt, and wearing it would make me feel better. I figured out that I'd semiconsciously imbued it with a magic that literally kept me from suicidal ideation. After that, I deliberately, consciously strengthened its borrowed power, and reaffirmed it every time I put it on. It wasn't the only thing I did to hold that in check, but it was one more useful brick in the wall.

Not every magical use of a T-shirt will be this dramatic, but it's still a great way to create a wearable spell. Try making your own with fabric paint. I was taught in my first coven that washing a garment removes all traces of magic and energy from it. I'm not sure how true this is in and of itself every time, but I know that a spell can be permanently incised on it with art and decoration that will resist all washings, trading with friends, et cetera. In ancient times, such spells would have been embroidered in with painstaking care. A T-shirt decal works just as well. I know a friend who made a stop-smoking spell by painting big, red, slashed circles over the logos on the Marlboro T-shirt handed down to her (like her smoking habit) from her father.

Part II: Body Modifications

Life is hard on a body. You can look at almost anyone from any walk of life, and inspect their body from head to toe, and one can't help but notice that no matter how cushy life is or isn't for someone, life leaves its marks, even in the twenty-first century. There are scars on almost anyone's body, big or small. Some people have massive scars from things like car accidents or falls. Some of them are not accidental; they are marks left by other people on purpose, either through acts of cruelty or negligence. Still others have scars and marks from medical treatment, such as surgeries or invaders into the body such as cancers, tumors, pieces of glass or metal—even vaccinations can leave scars.

And then there are those of us, especially in urban areas, who don't have very much that's permanent. We change apartments and jobs, maybe even friends, quite frequently. The only thing that really belongs to us in this life is our physical bodies (and some would argue we don't even own those), and some of us voluntarily mark or modify our bodies, sometimes for spiritual or magical reasons. I got my first piercing when I was fourteen, like many others: earrings. I'm a female in this culture, and it was very unusual when I was growing up not to have them done, sometimes when one was small or even an infant, non-consenting. By the time I was fourteen, I had mostly swallowed down the fear or the prick of that machine that piercers call—sometimes affectionately, sometimes derogatorily—a gun.

the piercing experience

It was important to me that my first body piercing experience be done not so much for marking an occasion, though it was a form of initiation, because I wanted somebody to do it who understood what it was like to be afraid for a very long time, and then to overcome that fear. My first ear piercings were done in a flea market in New Jersey by a very nice old biker in his sixties, and the reason I chose him to do it was because his wife had talked to me kindly. I kept asking her silly questions like, "Does it hurt?" and she shrugged and replied that she was quite the fraidy cat, and fingered her own earrings and told me that her husband had just done them about a month ago, and it wasn't bad, that she'd experienced much worse pain in her life.

At that time my only reason for wanting my ears pierced was simple: I wanted to be able to wear earrings! Specifically, I wanted one particular pair of earrings, emblazoned with symbols that I loved, symbols that would be hard to remove. I was so eager to wear these symbols that I started wearing them too soon for healing, and I suffered from bouts of painful infection for years until I was able to get proper jewelry for my ear holes. But even this early difficulty didn't stop me from continuing to get my body pierced; I ended up with two holes in one ear and three in the other, and decided to keep them that way. Why? Because life isn't balanced; it's rarely fair, so I put asymmetry in my ears to symbolize this. Life always leans a little bit to the left, so to speak—not in terms of evil, but a little of darkness, and mystery, and surprise. Five is a power number, like points in a pentagram. I wear hematite beads on them for power and potency.

After all the infections had cleared up, it occurred to me that my body was very sensitive. I suffer from all kinds of strange food allergies, and my body is not good at recovering from illness; I'm often the first to catch a cold and the last to get rid of it. So I vowed to make sure, from that time on, that my body really wanted the modifications that I was going to impose on it. I decided that if my body really wanted something done to it, it would tell me, and it does. The way it tells me that it wants different piercings or tattoos is through dreams—if I dream about getting one, I assume that it's either my body telling me that it wants one or a communication from a higher power making a firm suggestion to me.

For example, I'd wanted my nose pierced since I was nine and had seen it in *National Geographic* on some indigenous South Americans. I thought it was one of the most beautiful and striking piercings I'd ever seen up until that time, but it wasn't until I was twenty-three that I dreamed I had woken up from a very long sleep, not groggy but amazingly clear, and I had a pain in my nose. The feeling was oddly comforting and familiar, though, and I kept looking into the mirror and seeing this silvery steel ring in my nose. I dreamed that I was descending a long flight of steps, and on each of the steps was a different person in my life who had gotten in my way or put me down or somehow ebbed my confidence in myself or helped me to hurt my own self-esteem. As I went down, I looked each one of them in the eye and raised my hand, and they literally levitated off the stairway, swept out of my way into thin air. So to me the septum piercing that I got afterward is about power; about confronting obstacles in the form of other people, and not allowing my "face value" to others affect me to the point of not getting things done in my life.

The next major piercing I had done was a tongue piercing. I got this one done because I'm a very verbal person. There's an old, old Chinese legend about their hell—it was believed that people who had committed certain sins would be punished for them before they could go to the heavenly part of the Underworld. In the Confucian system, one of the major sins that a ruler or officer could perpetrate was telling lies or using their tongue to cause harm or damage to those beneath them, and the afterlife punishment for that was to have a nine-inch spike whacked through their tongue by one of the guardians of hell. Since speech is one of my gifts, and I value it, I put this bar in the center of my tongue to remind me of the power of my words, and how they reflect on my spirituality. Every time I move my mouth, it's there and I'm reminded not to lie or speak maliciously.

My labret (lower lip) piercing also came from a dream. I dreamed that I went into a shop but didn't have any money (which isn't an uncommon occurrence for me), and a friend of mine came in and smiled, and said, "Oh, you're here for your appointment?"

"No," I said. "I can't afford anything."

"No, it's time," he said. "We have to pierce you right now." And he did it, and I felt a sense of relief and well-being afterward.

My navel piercing came about because as a kid I always got strange pains and needle-like sensations in my navel area when I was upset or bored, as if evil spirits were pricking me inside with pins. I dreamed that I was at a large gathering and walked by the tent of an older woman I knew; she waved me in and told me that it was time for my first ceremony of womanhood, and pierced me with a porcupine quill. After I got the piercing some days later, I stopped getting those sharp feelings there altogether. The ring there is hung with rose quartz, chosen because it's the love stone. My belly has been a point of contention in my past; like most women, I don't have a washboard stomach and as a teenager I felt hateful toward my rounded, "imperfect" belly. The stone expresses love for my belly in spite of cultural demands that surround me, and helps with cramping.

All of my piercings except for the ears are in a straight line down the center of my body, and I think of it as my inner pole, a sense of balance and continuity in the body, echoing the line of chakras that runs from head to foot. The magic that I do with them is real; I focus on my tongue piercing, for instance, when I have to make a speech or say something difficult. I periodically take my jewelry out, smudge it with incense, pray for results, and replace it.

tattoos

I have over twenty tattoos on my body as well, acquired in a variety of settings, from professional tattooing parlors to "scratchers"—unlicensed beginners who do it for love or money. My most obvious one is on the back of my left hand, which like that of so many other people is my "off" hand. I think of it as the hand of latent memories, and I placed on it an old shield design from Nigeria that appeared in a book on Yoruba deities. I was at that time getting communications from an Orisha or deity named Eshu-Ellegua, who is a governor and keeper of the crossroads and the divine messenger, similar to Mercury/Hermes. The shield sign supposedly belonged to a "lost tribe" of Africa; apparently the neighboring peoples still see this symbol marked into stone or wood, but they claim to know nothing about the lost tribe's history. This is unusual, since the people that we know as the Yoruba and the tribes they conquered kept extensive oral histories that are still used, but this one tribe has been effectively erased from living memory, so that tattoo is a reminder to me of fate.

Over my left breast I have a picture of Chiron the centaur, teacher of many famous heroes, instructing a woman in the use of a lyre; it symbolizes lyrical poetry and the arts. I focus on this tattoo when I have to do a difficult artistic work. On my forearm is a sun with a running ibex in its heart; it is a personal symbol for my animus, my masculine energy that I work with spiritually when I need to. On my upper arm lies a Sphinx, adapted from the Wheel of Fortune card in the Rider-Waite Tarot; she carries a sword and is a charm of protection.

The Kundalini snake on my arm, curled up in a lotus, represents the Kundalini energy curled up at the base of the spine. I was doing Kundalini release work at the time, and when I work with that energy now I focus on this picture. Above that, on my arm, is a figure of Yemaya, the Ocean/Mother Goddess in Yoruba culture, holding a sacred mask and a serpent, representing the healing arts. It is there to honor her and to remind me to take it easy and be calm, regenerating myself. On my shoulder is a woman's head merging with an eagle's; this is in honor of a time when I was working with eagle power—the ability to fly high and see the bigger picture, both on a physical and a spiritual level, something very difficult for me. The image helps me to keep an eagle-eye perspective on things. On my other shoulder is a Horned God skull, symbolizing death and the spirits of the underworld; I focus on this in a mirror when I'm working with the death gods and their energy.

Other tattoos, such as my two Triple Goddess images on my back, are more "passive" magic—there to be a ward and guard, "watching" my back rather than being actively focused on at any time.

Obviously, like getting pierced, getting tattooed is an area where health is important. When checking out a tattoo parlor, look for cleanliness and hygienic practices. Ask a lot of questions—do they have an autoclave, do they use disposable needles, how do they dispose of waste, and so on. Find out what kind of inks are used. Some people may be allergic to artificial inks and prefer soy-based materials. Some people may be allergic to soy. If you're allergy-prone and aren't sure what to do, you may want to have one little dot tattooed on you somewhere unobtrusive and see how it behaves.

Don't just settle for some guy that you kind of know who has a tattoo kit in his bedroom. This goes for the heavier kinds of body modification as well, such as branding and dyed cuttings. We aren't going to go into the magical methods for these mods, because they are expensive and definitely acquired tastes, which most modern primitives aren't going to be interested in. However, the same safety issues go for all of them. If possible, ask for references. Find other people who have endured this artist's work, and look at what they've got. Ask about how they view the results. Compare to other people who've worked with other artists. Try to find out if your target artist has any unsatisfied customers, and why they're unsatisfied.

Tattooing is illegal in some states, so you may have to travel outside the state line to get one. Although we do believe that tattooing does have an unfair rap—most banning has less to do with safety issues and more to do with its disreputable old-time association with bars, prostitution, and drunken sailors—tattooists who work underground in illegal states often don't have the ability to set up really good, clean spaces like those of legal professionals. It may well be worth your time to cross state lines.

body-modification ceremonies

I have presided, if you will, over several different ritual body modification ceremonies other than my own, and they've all been powerful experiences. Helping someone set up a life-changing ceremony is life-changing for the priest/ess as well. Sometimes, if the piercer/tattooer/brander/cutter isn't clear on what you want for your ritual body modification, it may help to bring in a more experienced pagan, perhaps a clergy member, who has had ritual body mods done to themselves or else helped with someone else's, and who can advocate for you and help to work out what you want in such a way that it does not interfere with the artist's work. Remember that once you've done this yourself, you will become one of those experienced pagans who can help others in this way. Let it be known in the community that you're willing to do this, as a kind of offering back to the gods.

If you're a clergy member (or even just a trusted friend) who's been asked to help with something like this, remember that there may be some actual pain involved—how much will depend on the specific procedure and the person's pain tolerance. You and the client need to discuss what s/he will say to stop things if the pain gets too intense, and what you both will do together to calm him/her in order to continue. If the client has no experience with pain management, it might be worth your time to look into the breathing exercises used by prepared childbirth classes, and go over them beforehand—yes, even for male clients. You need to stay calm and not be empathically ruffled by the client's struggles; they are depending on you to be their calm center to lean on, and the artist may be depending on you to keep them calm so that they can focus on doing a good job with their work. Work on breathing exercises for yourself as well. Find out what sort of thing calms the client in terms of scents, colors, temperature, and physical sensation—will a physical touch calm or upset them, and where? What sort of cleansing will they want first, and can it be done at the studio, or at home? Find out about aftercare of the wound from the piercer, and make sure that it gets done before any final ritual happens.

The first body modification ritual that I helped with still stays with me, in my mind. I was asked for help by Jason, a piercer friend of mine who was doing a branding/cutting with an electric scalpel. A female client was getting a Triple Goddess incised on her outer thigh in order to dedicate herself to Her, and Jason asked me to help her prepare the space, feeling that another pagan woman present would make her feel more comfortable. Since the space where the cutting was done had to be thoroughly sterilized, I felt that a ritual bath would be in order. It would cleanse both the body and the aura, and calm her, and be a way to honor her body. Since she was a former sex abuse victim with size issues, I felt that creating a space where her body would be honored was important. I set about preparing the bathroom by first insisting that it be completely clean from top to bottom beforehand, and then smudged the room first with dragon's blood for purification and then with frankincense to bring in light and solar energies. I placed a large white candle on top of the toilet tank and surrounded it with fresh and false flowers, because it was the most visible focal point of the room. On the four corners of the tub we placed alternating blue and white votive candles—white for purification and the color of the moon, and blue for tranquility.

When the woman arrived, I helped to disrobe her and smudged her with white sage and lavender as a form of gentle cleansing for her aura. While she bathed, I lit floral incenses that she had chosen in honor of her goddess within—rose, jasmine, and violet. We had put sea salt, rosemary, rose petals, thyme, and jasmine oil in her bath, and took special time to repeatedly wash the area where the mark would be made, and discussed its significance. As a priestess, I was asked to bless that part of her body before the branding commenced.

While this was going on, my friend the piercer was preparing his space, smudging the air with white sage, and covering the padded bench she would be lying on with his altar cloth, which was decorated with a celestial pattern. After the bath was finished, I wrapped her in a robe and escorted her to the area where she would be marked. She recited a prayer she'd written to the Goddess, and her personal vows to Her. I laid a blessing on Jason, his hands, his equipment, and the machine. The branding/cutting itself took about forty-five minutes to finish, from antiseptic to cleanup. She was very happy, both with her cutting and with the whole experience, and for me it was one of the best ritual experiences I've ever helped with.

piercing magic

The useful thing about body modification magic is that it's something you can't lose; it would have to be ripped out or sliced away from your body. Also, some piercings and tattoos are very easy to hide. There's no threat of leaving them in a restroom or on someone's dining room table; most don't even have to be removed during a shower. Although this book can give you ideas for ritual uses, please consult with a reputable piercer for health risks and appropriate jewelry. Putting holes in yourself is a high-risk activity. Please don't do this at home. People have severely injured themselves from secondary infections due to low sterility. If you are under eighteen, it is highly unlikely that you will find a reputable piercer willing to do anything more than ear or possibly side-nose piercing, because you are unable to legally consent and they can legally be sued if your parents have a problem with your piercings.

See page 142 on piercing safety and rights before you go any further. This will help you decide whether a piercer is responsible and trustworthy. Although many piercers are simply in it for the fun of it, there are more and more piercers all the time who will do their work in a ritual setting for magical and/or ceremonial purposes. Ask around carefully. If this piercing will be important to you for more than just mere decoration, you deserve more than just a perfunctory job in the back of someone's store with no creation of sacred space or respect for your feelings. Be a good consumer; ask questions and carefully explain what it is that you want. Don't beat around the bush. You need someone who will understand your needs and be willing to go along with them, even if you insist on playing Bobby McFerron music really loud and smudging the room with asafoetida.

Fifty years ago, the only piercings anyone ever saw were in people's earlobes, but now many people can walk the street with more exotic piercings, and modern primitives come up with more and more places to put holes in all the time. We're listing the piercings that have become "traditional" in the last fifteen years in the modern primitive community; there are stranger and more exotic ones coming out all the time, but these tend to be more dangerous and complicated, and are usually beyond the means of the average urban primitive, who can neither afford the monetary nor the physical output. If you're interested in such extremities, please check out any of the fine body modification magazines in circulation, or the online Body Modification Ezine (www.bme.freeq.com).

RITUAL PIERCING LIST

Ears. Long known as a rite of passage, ear piercing is the most common and unobtrusive body modification. In both ancient societies and the modern pagan community, it has been and is used as part of a puberty rite. Many male-to-female transsexuals that I know got their ears pierced as kind of a "second puberty" rite, as a formal way of beginning their transition to female. Sailors who'd been around the world the long way, under the tips of Africa and South America, would get an earring in remembrance of it. It's usually a person's first piercing, and more often than not it's done with a semi-sanitary gun quickly in some shop, and usually to a kid. When your child wants earrings, you should find them a real piercer to do it with a needle and not a gun. Needles are sharp and pierce; guns create ragged puncture wounds that don't heal as fast or as cleanly, and due to body fluids getting onto the gun, they are never as sterile as a single-use needle. You should also encourage your child to get the earrings in honor of some actual event—perhaps puberty, or graduation from a particular grade with good marks, or doing part of the Appalachian Trail, or losing a friend or relative to death, or the breakup of their first real relationship. Piercings can commemorate hard ordeals as well as good experiences; the idea is that you survived, and are stronger and more adult now that you're through it. Even if your child is iffy about big rituals, they can understand the concept of a memorial reward.

Eyebrow. Associated with the sun. This is a difficult piercing, because it is against the orbital bone and is a surface-to-surface wound that tends to grow out on some people. You have to be careful not to lay wrong on it, or you'll give yourself headaches. However, since it is near the eyes, the brow piercing is used for the magic of seeing clearly. It is especially good for people who tend to be overwhelmed by their feelings and have trouble being objective. This piercing is the "bird's eye" modification, which can give you the fly-high-see-far, long-term view. It can also be used magically to allow one to see through the eyes of other animals, if you hang a charm on it carved into the animal of your choice.

Nose. There are two kinds of nose piercings; the side nose, which is more common, and the septum, which goes through the piece of cartilage between the nostrils. Side-nose piercings are considered more feminine (although we've seen a few men wearing them), and septum piercings are considered more masculine (although we've seen a few women wearing them). Young women in India have been getting decorative side-nose piercings for years, long before we in the West ever started, usually for weddings, betrothals, coming-of-marriageable-age, or other mating-related reasons. This piercing is associated with goddesses of love and fertility, whose provenance is beauty, attraction, and creating relationships. It is associated with both Venus and Jupiter, whose wife was Juno/Hera, Goddess of Marriage. Wearing it advertises on a magical level that you are of age to consider (or perhaps are already in) serious sexual and emotionally-committed relationships with some degree of permanence. If you're still in the wildly dating, no-commitment stage, you may want to reconsider this piercing. If you already have it and want to counteract its magical effects, use a very small stud, perhaps with a "no" stone (see chart below). Wearing a chain between your side-nose piercing and earring is referred to as a "suicide chain," due to its drawbacks during street fighting. It implies extreme vulnerability, which is perhaps something that some people might like to advertise in certain bars and clubs when looking for a dominant, protective, potential mate, but may give the wrong idea on the street or at work. Be judicious.

Septum. Septum piercings are honorable warrior piercings, associated with Mars. Warriors are not berserkers. They have rules and codes of honorable behavior, and thus the ring at the very center of their visage states that they are willing to be "ring led" by those rules, allowing their strength and power to be bound to the service of a greater power. The ring on the nose is associated with rings placed in the noses of pigs, bears, and other large and destructive animals in order to control them.

By wearing the warrior's ring in your nose, you advertise that you are strong enough not to need to prove your strength with random violence; that you have self-control and are not afraid to go into battle with the handicap either of that piercing or of your restraining code of rules.

Lip. This piercing either rings around or studs through the soft tissue at either side of your lip. Associated with Mercury and Saturn, as these piercings are used magically to limit your speech and make you careful of what you say. This is one of the easier piercings to screw up on because piercers can put it too far down the lip and create a swollen look. Because of the "fish-hook" appearance that the lip-ring piercing has, it can be used to magically indicate a strong attachment to someone, perhaps a wedding, handfasting, or betrothal sort of piercing.

Labret. Usually a stud piercing through the central lower lip, in the cleft between the chin and lip. This is a traditional piercing of certain Northwest Coast Indian tribes, used by women in positions of authority. As they grew older and passed menopause, they would get larger and larger plugs to show their age and the respect that they deserved. For a woman, this is a very matriarchal piercing, but for either gender it suggests authority, experience, and status as an important person to one's tribe. Unlike piercings that are youthful rites of passage, this one magically advertises a need to take on more responsibility to one's peers, and if you get a labret too young, you may well find your freedom going mysteriously down the tubes, and new and challenging tasks that require hard work and steadiness appearing to weigh you down. Be careful what you ask for.

Tongue. This piercing is usually a barbell through the tongue; the ones further back are harder to see and more discreet. There are two kinds of barbells; one with threaded holes in the balls and threaded ends on the stem that they screw onto, and one with threaded holes in the ends of the stem and threaded stubs on the balls that screw into them. The second variety is unsafe for use as a tongue piercing, as there has been at least one reported fatality due to someone swallowing the ball, whose tiny stub tore through his intestines and caused peritonitis. Teens should be cautious about tongue piercings, because they can chip the enamel on still-growing teeth.

Tongue piercings are anti-lying spells, associated with Mercury and Saturn, the planet of communication and the planet of obstacles. As discussed, the Chinese believe that public liars are sent to a hell after death where great spikes are hammered through their tongues, and public officials in certain primitive tribes get tongue piercings to remind them not to lie to their people. Tongue piercings are useful for those who constantly tell small white lies (or big ones) or continually exaggerate, often more out of habit than anything else.

Nipples. This is either a solar or lunar piercing, depending on whether you think of your nipples as being attached to a "chest" or "breasts." If you associate them with the terms "pectorals," "strong," and "muscular," it's solar. If you associate them with the terms "beautiful," "nurturing," and/or "sensual," it's lunar. The metal of the piercing, and any stones or pendants, should reflect this choice. Either way, they are used to give "heart," however you may imply that. There is more than one kind of courage. Solar courage implies the ability to do, to make decisions, to be confident of one's choices. Lunar courage implies being brave enough to be vulnerable, to face and express one's feelings openly, to dare to trust. Nipple piercings on women should be removed during pregnancy and lactation, because irritation may ensue as the breasts go through many changes.

Navel. This is a fertility piercing for women, associated with the moon, and used to invoke balancing feminine energy for men. Navel piercings are good for women who want to have children, advertise their ability to have children, or honor their childbearing years. Ironically, if you actually get pregnant, you may have to take your navel piercing out toward the end of your gestation, since the navel extends and irritation may occur. Most people think about belly dancers when they think navel piercing; the flashing jewel in the belly that glitters with hip-swaying movements. Middle Eastern belly dancing was originally a women's fertility dance, performed the night before a wedding to ensure easy childbearing. A man who gets a navel piercing can invoke the power of an "astral womb" into himself, releasing his anima, or female side. These piercings should be pampered while healing—wear your waistbands well below them. In fact the best thing to wear while a navel piercing is healing is nothing at all with a waistband; something long and loose and flowing, which further magically reinforces the female energy as well as alleviates possible irritation. Women with large bellies, and issues about them, may want to get a navel piercing as part of a magical working to learn to love their bodies. However, large bellies also need extra care with regard to proper healing due to rolls of fat that crease, so keep this in mind and pamper that lovely tummy properly.

Genitals, Female. You can get rings in your inner or outer labia, a ring or barbell through your clitoral hood, or even one through the shaft of the clitoris itself, although many piercers will not perform this last one for fear of damaging nerve endings in the tiny and tightly packed clitoris. Associated, of course, with Venus. The most common ritual use I've seen yet for female genital piercing of any kind is a reclaiming ceremony after some kind of abuse—rape, sexual molestation, or just the continual onslaught of harmful social messages that discourage young women from owning, loving, and making their own decisions about their own organs. By getting a genital piercing, these women give themselves a solid reminder that no one else can force them to do anything sexual that they do not desire, and if they are forced against their will through greater strength and cruelty, no fault or blame falls to them. Some use it openly as an anti-rape spell, others simply as a reminder and sign of self-acceptance.

Genitals, Male. Lots of different ones here. Penis piercings consist of the Prince Albert (a ring through the urethra and underside of the head), ampallang (sideways barbell through the head), apadravya (vertical, up-and-down barbells through the shaft), and dydoes (little rings lined up along the top edge of the helmet). These are associated with Mars the protector of male sexuality rather than Mars the warrior, and with Pan. Many men use such piercings to dedicate themselves to some code of sexual or gender-role behavior—perhaps a commitment to accepting their sexuality or sexual preference, or committing to a particular lover, or to their own personal code of manhood, which may or may not be congruent with social expectation.

Scrotum. Scrotum piercings are concerned with male fertility rather than specifically sexuality, and are associated with Jupiter, the planet of abundance, due to the abundant levels of sperm secreted by the average male. The hafada, which is a ring through the scrotal skin around the testicle, was originally used as a puberty rite by certain African and Arab tribesmen, in order that the newly descended testicles not work their way back up into the body cavity. The coolness of the metal may actually help keep the scrotum cool and sperm count up. It's a useful virility spell for men who lack confidence in their ability to sire children or perform sexually. A ring or band around the top of the scrotum, where it attaches to the body—which may or may not be an actual piercing—can be used as an anti-fertility spell, as a way of beseeching the gods to prevent pregnancies. Please don't depend on it solely, though . . . wear that latex!

Guiche. The final common genital piercing, which is usually worn by men but has very rarely been seen on women, is the guiche. This is a ring attached to the perineum, the area of skin between genitals and anus. Positioned close to the anal sphincter, it is associated with Pluto, which rules elimination and letting go, and Saturn, which rules boundaries and obstacles. It is used ritually to symbolize sexual limitations one has consented to take on, such as a vow of celibacy, monogamy, or specific codes of sexual behavior. The idea is that one limits certain activities, and lets go of unacceptable desires.

TYPES OF BODY MODIFICATION JEWELRY

Captive bead rings. First and most common are captive bead rings. This is a ring with a small break in it that can be put through a hole in your body. A bead is then slipped through the break to close the ring. Beads can be made out of any variety of materials—metal, bone, semiprecious stone, or plastic. Charms can be slid onto a captive bead ring as well, as long as they have a hole or jump ring to hang from.

Stones. These are one of the most common types of piercing charms. Semiprecious are most common; if you want to frequent the really good piercing shops and spend lots of money, you can even come up with precious stones. You can get a small bead in almost any stone you can think of, especially if you go to gem and mineral shows. You can even get them in shapes other than round, such as cylindrical, cubical, pyramidal, or carved to represent small animals.

Horseshoe. Another common piercing is the horseshoe, which is shaped just like that, with a bead on each end. Horseshoes are most often put through septums (the central cartilage of your nose between your nostrils, the classic "bone through the nose" piercing), nipples, or possibly earlobes. They can theoretically be put anywhere that a ring can go, but since it's open at the end of the arch, there's more risk of getting it caught on something.

Barbell. Another style is the barbell. This is a straight rod of various lengths with a bead on each end. The safest variety has threads on either end, and the balls have threaded holes that screw onto it. Barbells are popular in tongues, eyebrows, certain penile piercings, and occasionally in nipples.

Spikes. These are solid needles, usually tapered at both ends, made of various materials such as surgical steel, gold, plastic, or natural materials such as bone, bamboo, or porcupine quills. They can range from an inch to as much as a foot wide. They are usually put through the septum, because the middle of your face is about the only place where you can keep them without interference. We've seen them occasionally in nipples, but only in instances where the person doesn't have to wear a shirt.

Plugs. Once worn by the ancient Aztecs and Mayans, plugs are generally for stretched piercings. A plug is an edged cylinder made of metals, woods, bone, acrylic, or stone. A plug requires a much larger hole, and one generally starts with a small piercing and slowly stretches it wider with larger and larger jewelry over time. Patience is of the essence. The drawback to plugs is that once you get a hole of a certain size, it's permanent. Unlike small piercing holes, which will close up with time, a plug-size hole will be with you forever, short of surgical correction, so be careful before you choose this option.

PRECIOUS AND SEMIPRECIOUS STONES FOR PIERCING JEWELRY

Many piercing rings come with small precious or semiprecious stones as captive beads or pendants, and they lend their particular energy to the magic of the piercing itself. These can be adapted to alter or further aim the magic of the charm. We list the most popular ones here.

Agate. An earthy stone, in earthy colors. Used to give appetite, heal illnesses, and make one more in tune with the Earth and nature.

Amber. Solar stone, actually petrified resin, gives courage and self-confidence, makes one feel secure in one's chosen identity.

Amethyst. Calms, soothes, and helps you to overcome addictions, especially alcoholism. Good stone for AA members to wear on their persons at all times, and for anyone trying to break a bad habit.

Aventurine. The money stone, green with gold flecks. For money and financial help.

Bloodstone. The stone of nobility or, these days, of the executive. In ancient times, only nobles could wear it. Gives the ability to manage resources and people well and efficiently, and inspire leadership.

Carnelian. The lust stone, from the Latin *carne*, meaning "flesh." Adds libido and vital energy. Especially good for nipple and genital piercings. Associated with both Venus and Mars together.

Citrine. A form of yellow quartz, it's good for protection and energy. Solar stone.

Clear quartz. Water magic, sacred to Neptune, as quartz was thought to be solidified water or ice. Tumbled clear quartz is good for washing away long-held and soured negative emotions. Quartz crystals are good "memory" keepers; just visualize what you want and "zap" it in. They can be pretty all-purpose. Smoky quartz helps you to see what is obscured, and the lighter varieties give clarity of mind and spirit. The rutilated variety helps to calm mental illness.

Coral. Sacred to the Sea Mother, coral represents deep nurturing and maternal care.

Diamond. The hardest stone of all, its energy symbolizes loyalty and perseverance, thus its inclusion in wedding rings. (Oddly enough, it is not a love stone, just a loyalty stone.) Can be used to mark any vow that you really want to be able to keep.

Emerald. The ultimate Earth stone, sacred to Mother Gaea. Expensive, but a direct line to her. Wear in order to tap into the pure energy of Earth to refresh yourself.

Fluorite. The student stone. Good for school, learning, taking tests, and retaining taught information. Keeps wits sharp and focus intent. Sacred to Mercury.

Garnet. Another Mars-associated courage stone. Romans put them in sword hilts, both for bravery in battle and to stanch blood. Wear to help ongoing anemia. Called the "old maid" stone; especially good for people who choose to live alone with no partners (or have to do so for periods of time) and have to fend for and stand up for themselves.

Hematite. The ultimate grounding stone. Put a necklace of hematite around your neck, and you'll probably get the immediate urge to lie down. Grounds any area of the body it is placed on. Good for flighty, nervous, disconnected people; used to help seizure disorders. A Saturn stone.

Jade. The Chinese called it the King of Heaven and claimed it brought longevity, even unto immortality. Good for health problems in the kidneys, liver, and intestines.

Jasper. Both the red and green varieties and the leopard variety are sacred to Mars, but with an earthy feel. As such, they give energy and the ability to act, but in practical, everyday matters. Good for people who have a hard time remembering to pay the rent, confronting their boss, calling the electric company, looking for work, eating right, and otherwise taking care of physical needs in a timely and efficient manner.

Jet. The gem of night, jet is fossilized wood that is closely related to coal. Pair with amber to create an energy of equal day and night. Used for seeing in the dark and understanding the gods of night, silence, darkness, and mystery. Associated with Saturn.

lapis lazuli. Stone of the sky gods. Used for any spell regarding the intellect—mental strength, clarity, inspiration, imagination, the ability to think quickly and deeply. Can bring out the divine nature of the mind. Good for philosophers. Associated with Mercury and Jupiter.

Malachite. Stone of the magician. A highly powerful stone, not to be used for magic by beginners. Associated with Pluto, the planet of destruction and regeneration, malachite will trigger backlogs of karma and quicken your action-consequence rebound. Used for deep psyche work, and shamanic work when the entire life needs to be reexamined, and possibly discarded and started over. As it contains copper arsenate, do not wear it in or near your mouth where you could chew on it.

Moonstone. Stone, of course, of the moon. Good for female puberty rite jewelry, women's reproductive health, pregnancy, abortion or miscarriage aftercare, and for anyone of any gender coping with overwhelming emotions, such as the birth of a child, a new change in life, or the death of a loved one. Its lunar energies are soothing and calming and promote emotional growth.

Obsidian. One of the "no" stones, associated with Saturn. Negates the ritual meaning or intent of the jewelry. On its own, can be used for setting boundaries and refusing to do something.

Onyx. The stone of the Demon Within. Used for working with one's fears and inner monsters, learning to accept and love them, and possibly learning to heal them, a process that must be done in that order. Shadow work, associated with Pluto. Use with care.

Opal. Stone of the mirror. Used to bring out inner beauty; as such, good for parts of the body you perceive as unbeautiful. Associated with Neptune; it gives a boost to the imagination and is good for writer's or artist's block.

Pearl. Sacred to the Sea Mother and the Moon Goddess (often the same deity), pearls are linked to the physical female mysteries and can be worn to affirm womanhood or to heal trouble with the female organs. Can be worn by men to remind them of one particular woman, or of the Goddess.

Ruby. Protective, and expensive. Gives heat—good for people with poor circulation who are always cold. Helps to manage and express repressed anger. Sun/Mars feel to it.

Rose Quartz. The love stone, sacred to Venus. Used on any part of the body that you are uncomfortable with and wish to learn to love. Also given as love gifts, and to children to keep them feeling safe and loved.

Sapphire. Sacred to Uranus, sapphire is good for promoting honesty and harmony in any relationship, not just romantic ones but friends, associates, and those involved with you in group activities. Protective, not of people, but of causes and goals. Expensive.

Sodalite. Stone of the messenger, flying high and seeing far. Will give alertness and ability to see opportunities, and sharpens the intellect. Associated with Mercury.

Tiger's-Eye. A courage stone for a warrior. The green version, cat's-eye, and the blue version, hawk's-eye, give courage in the fields of academia and politics, respectively.

Topaz. Invisibility and protection. Will let you walk unchallenged and unnoticed.

Tourmaline. A neutral stone whose use varies with its color—pink acts like rose quartz but is not as delicate, green acts as a healer, black as a binding Saturn stone, blue for de-stressing, and tourmalinated quartz for astral travel.

Turquoise. Safety in travel. Those constantly in transit or who spend a lot of time on road trips might do well to wear turquoise. Be careful not to be fooled by the fake turquoise sometimes offered for sale in many stores; it's really dyed howlite. Real turquoise should have a soapy, waxy feel to it, not hard and shiny. If you find fake turquoise being advertised as real, complain to the store manager.

Zircon. Another "no" stone that will negate the meaning of the jewelry. Use carefully.

Yes, these aren't all the ones in the world, but they are most of the common ones you'll find in the average jewelry shop. Of course, everything said here goes for non-piercing jewelry as well.

the piercee's bill of rights

Written by Jim Ward and Michaela Grey of the Gauntlet as a free donation to the piercing community.

Every person being pierced has the right . . .

1. *To be pierced in a scrupulously hygienic, open environment by a clean, conscientious piercer wearing a fresh pair of disposable latex or plastic gloves.*
2. *To a sober, friendly, calm, and knowledgeable piercer who will guide them through their piercing experience with confidence and assurance.*
3. *To the peace of mind that comes from knowing their piercer knows and practices the very highest standards of sterilization and hygiene.*
4. *To be pierced with a brand-new, completely sterilized needle, which is immediately disposed of in a medical sharps container after use on the piercee alone.*
5. *To be touched only with freshly sterilized, appropriate implements, properly used and disposed of or resterilized in an autoclave prior to use on anyone else.*
6. *To know that ear-piercing guns are NEVER appropriate and are often dangerous when used on anything other than ear lobes.*
7. *To be fitted with jewelry that is appropriately sized, safe in material, design, and construction, and which best promotes healing. Gold-plated, gold-filled, and sterling silver jewelry are never appropriate for any new or unhealed piercing.*
8. *To be fully informed about proper aftercare, and to have access to their piercer for further information about care.*

Remember: Safety before all else! A piercing can always be redone later, but health complications from infection can have far-reaching results. When in doubt, take it out!

twelve

Offspring

URBAN PAGAN CHILDREN

• • Perhaps the most fragile denizens of the city are the ones who did not choose to live there, and who have the least capacity to deal with its vagaries: human young. If you're an urban primitive with kids—and many are—you may be constantly worried for their safety. You may berate yourself, and be subtly berated by others, for requiring your children (usually for economic reasons) to live in the city, especially if circumstances force you into an area that is less than completely safe. Although you may pile on the protective magic, your kids will eventually step out the door—to school, to the neighbor's, to a friend's—or, in the case of older kids, all over town. The answer is not to barricade them in as if you were all living in the proverbial tiny cottage at the edge of the vast, untenanted forests of European fairy tales; nor, in the case of older kids, is it to chaperone them everywhere. Children have to leave the nest and spread their wings, if only in small ways. Your protective magic needs to follow them wherever they go, keeping them safe on the move.

Protective Spells for Kids

With small children, it's easy to put a protective amulet on them, as they aren't likely to either figure it out or be embarrassed. Stickers or decals, of symbols that are symbolic of strength and protection to your inner self, are good things to slap on lunch boxes or knapsacks or the covers of schoolbooks. We personally find the psychedelic ones that have a spiral pattern on them to be effective, and kids love them.

You can make an amulet to attach to the child's coat (tongue of zipper or end of drawstring) from Fimo, one of many oven-hardening polymer clays, or from a painted wooden bead, or a pendant. A tiny mojo bag of herbs is all right if you're sure your child is past the stage where they'll put things in their mouth.

Protection spells can also be painted on the soles of a child's shoes. Sneakers are best for this, as they're reasonably flat, and even the treads can be painted on. Use house paint, which will take a while to wear off. Actually it doesn't matter if the paint wears off, because you're charging the shoe itself as you paint. Imagine burning a brand onto it that will last forever. You can make a big, pale grey spot for invisibility while walking through difficult areas, and a red spear or sword for protection against attacks. Older kids may not be so happy about you painting up their shoes; use your judgment and ask them. If the kid is enthused about the idea, you can even extend the paint onto the sneaker uppers—Raven's daughter decorated hers with "puffy paints" from the craft store. Painting wings on the upper heels will insure speed and agility if your child has to run for their safety, and an arrow on the toe keeps them from getting lost or sidetracked.

If you're worried about your child getting lost frequently, make an amulet with the symbol of a spider in a web. The spider leaves its web only on a line of silk that it can quickly run back up again if necessary. Picture your love as that line of silk, drawing your child back home. If you're more worried about physical attacks, paint the amulet white or light grey and imbue it with an invisibility spell (see chapter 3, Defenses).

Take a photo of your child, along with a little of their hair, and place it in a jar. Then fill the jar with salt and spices, and picture them being safe and sound. A similar spell can be done for a child who is sad or depressed, assuming that everything that can be done toward the cause of that sorrow has been done. Rub something sweet, such as honey or sugar water, over the mouth of the picture, that they might taste only sweetness. Then, instead of salt, fill the jar with flower petals. A good place to get flower petals for free in the city is the dumpsters behind florist shops; you can stop in periodically, pluck the petals off of the bruised and bedraggled flowers they abandon, and leave them to dry at home in a sieve or plastic net bag such as onions are sold in. When you have enough, fill the jar, cap it, and put it in a warm place. Make sure that the petals are thoroughly dry, however, or they'll mold.

nightmares

One of the biggest problems a small child can have is nightmares. Kids pick up more than grownups think they do, and they store the various stresses they encounter in their subconscious, where they can spring forth as bad dreams. The very first spell that Raven taught his daughter to do was the banishing of bad dreams; a kid as young as four can do it. Raven hung a paper cutout on each of her walls: a white cloud puff with a sun peeking out in the east, a bonfire in the south, a blue wave in the west, and a tree in the north. (This is a great way to familiarize any kid with the elements anyhow.) Then he got her a "magic wand"—in this case it was one of those plastic tubes filled with fluid and glitter, but a magic wand can be handmade from any stick and decorated with anything. He taught her to wave the wand in each of the four directions, and then up and down, each time saying "Nothing can harm me!" This ritual could be performed in the evening before going to bed, or in the middle of the night when she woke up from a bad dream. It gives kids some sense of power, some ability to affect what is troubling them; if you feel stronger and safer, you sleep easier.

Another good folk anti-nightmare spell requires four horseshoes (they don't have to be real, you can cut them out of cardboard) that you place under each edge of the bed, facing outward. This way the nightmare can only run away from the bed, instead of coming toward it. Another good trick is the dreamcatcher, which is available in all sorts of gift stores these days. They are hung over the head of the bed. As suggested in the Defenses chapter, a bag of cotton balls can be used for a spell to sleep as if on peaceful clouds.

Still another method utilizes the concept of the gargoyle. The point of having all those ugly gargoyles on churches is to ward off evil spirits, and to a child, that's what nightmares are: evil spirits. Go to the toy store and find four of the ugliest toy creatures you can find. They don't have to be large; rubber spiders and snakes work fine. Affix them to the four corners of the bed, and have your child touch each one and order it to guard them from random evil nasties. You'd be surprised what sort of grotesqueries even a retiring child will enthusiastically greet if they are sure the critters are "on their side."

making friends

If your child is having trouble making friends in school, you can create a "friend magnet." This is an easy one to do with your kid. Get a small refrigerator magnet—if you can't find a blank one, peel the stuff off of an old, cheap one. Then cut two hands out of leather, felt, or heavy fabric, and glue them to the magnet so that the fingers interlace. Visualize your child making friends and connections. This should be carried to school by your child each day.

If you have the kind of kid that just doesn't make friends easily, or doesn't get along with other kids, or doesn't fit in, you can do the gold mask spell. However, this spell should only be done if the child not only agrees and consents to it, but is enthusiastic about the idea. Not all loners should be forced to be popular, and in some school environments popularity can only come at the expense of one's integrity. A child who is continually the class scapegoat is suffering from a bad situation that is inherently unfair, and needs protection spells, not fitting-in spells. Possibly even justice spells directed at the schoolchildren or the administration might be in order, if you think it is warranted. If fitting in is less important to your child than being true to themselves, commend them for their integrity and do what you can to protect them from the evils of conformist retribution. They'll grow up to be adults who do not give in to threats and stand up for themselves.

On the other hand, if your child really wants to be popular and is just shy, or lacking in a few social graces, and is pleased by the idea of a popularity spell, you can try this one. Get a plastic or stiffened fabric mask from the store—they're everywhere at Halloween, but you can still get them at craft stores at other times of the year. If you're impoverished, you can probably trashpick them just after Halloween when people discard their costumes. Try not to start with one that's an ugly monster; you want a human face or at least a plain mask. You can make one yourself out of leather or two layers of heavy felt; make the nose out of a separate piece. Whatever you do, the mask should fit on your child's face without interfering in any way with their breathing, since being "suffocated" is a bad omen. This may require you to cut the nostrils further open. Paint it shiny gold, or cover it with gold fabric. Add sequins, feathers, anything you like. Go outside and hold it up to the sun to catch the light. Then hang it over your child's bed on a hook or nail.

Every morning, they should remove it from the wall, put it on, look in a mirror and say, "I shine brighter than the sun, and everyone will be drawn toward my glow." Then hang it back up and go off. It may take a week or so to get going, but we've had it work with quite a few kids. On the other hand, let your child know that if this morning ritual ever begins to feel uncomfortable for some reason, or strangely "not right," it is their psyche telling them that they are sacrificing some part of themselves for popularity, hiding their true selves. In that case, they should stop immediately and put the mask away.

city spirits

When your child is old enough to understand, you might also take them on a tour of the city and introduce them to the various city spirits. They may bond to some immediately and not be too fond of others; no one gets along with everyone. This can be useful as, if they're ever in an unsafe situation, such as being chased by other kids with hostile intent, and they are in the territory of one of the city spirits whom they have been introduced to and consider a friend, they can ask for emergency help or protection. Raven used to walk to high school through a wooded park; he was often caught and beaten up by other kids intent on punishing a scapegoat. Eventually he thought of asking the spirit of the park to help him out, and the attacks decreased dramatically—in fact, the kids often seemed to walk right by without noticing him while in the confines of the park.

Of course, such help should be paid for with offerings of thanks. Raven periodically left bread crumbs for the birds and wildlife, and when the spirit was eventually killed (the city decided to tear up the park and build a hydroelectric plant), he organized a wake, with friends, candles, and a mourning vigil.

thirteen

InterTribal Communication

HOW TO NOT START WARS

• • A number of years ago, Tannin was using a storage room in a Jamaican friend's botanica for a Tarot reading room. Tannin asked her if it would be all right to cleanse the room with incense after she set up the furniture. When she agreed, Tannin went about the work, and took it upon herself to begin cleaning not just the room, but the landing and stairway outside, where there was a large altar to Santa Barbara, the Santerían "alter ego" of Shango, the Orisha of Fire. Tannin was surprised when her friend came up the stairs and stopped her with a sharp word. She told her that it didn't matter what Tannin did with her own space, but not to mess with hers. Tannin was slightly stunned, murmured an apology, and retreated back into the reading room.

Unfortunately, in many of the Neopagan circles we've traveled in, there is an assumption of universality of intent; i.e., the idea that anything done with good intentions shouldn't be harmful. However, terminology is not the only thing that varies among different spiritual paths. In the above case, Tannin didn't think about the fact that the host had spent a lot of time and effort constructing a space of energy that would serve as the home of a particular deity, and she was interfering with that energy.

The concept that deities are archetypes, or powerful ideas, is hardly universal. A majority of the polytheists on this planet see them as real, living beings, as real as our neighbors—perhaps more so. Relations with them are bound by specific rules of courtesy that to violate would vary from rude to inexcusable. Tannin's offense wasn't of interference so much as discourtesy; her friend was not concerned about Shango being harmed in any way, but rather of having his privacy invaded. You wouldn't want anyone to come into your house without asking, vacuum your floors, and move around your furniture; neither does a god.

Every large (and even not-so-large) city is home to a variety of people from every corner of the world, each with their own unique religious practices and beliefs. It is not necessary to study all or any of them in detail, so long as you follow these simple rules of courtesy.

Rules of Courtesy

don't mess with someone else's ritual space

This includes altars, rituals, sacred objects and tools, and anything that you suspect might be one of these things. Some cultures practice making impromptu altars, offerings, or spells that they then leave in public or semi-public areas, such as along roadsides or at crossroads. Don't touch. Just because someone left an interesting thing by the road does not mean it is all right for you to take it. Courtesy aside, it isn't very wise to get drawn into the unknown spellwork of a stranger. By virtue of taking it into your home, you are bringing along whatever it means and was meant to do. If you aren't sure what it is, leave it.

The sole exception to this rule is if you find it on your own property. Whether it was put there unwittingly or knowingly, that is an invasion of your turf and you have the right to remove, destroy, or keep it, or whatever you like.

you are not the occult police

Sometimes, a Pagan or occult group, in the fervor of their new beliefs (and this usually happens to people who are newly come to magic), decide that they are the Occult Police, and they go out of their way to Stop Magical Wrongdoing wherever they think they see it, whether it's the upside-down pentagram spray-painted under an underpass by all the broken beer bottles, or a few scattered animal bones in an outlying wasteland. They eagerly smudge and chant their way to righteously erase all traces of such "evil" energy from the pristine Earth.

Don't do this. This is not your job. Those bones might be the remains of someone's beloved pet, or a roadkill that just wants to be left in peace. And wouldn't you just feel silly if the cops stopped and asked you what you were doing, chanting and burning funny-smelling stuff in that space where underage drinkers were partying the night before?

Seriously, it's easy to misunderstand and jump to conclusions when confronted with symbols and practices that are alien to us. We all, as humans, have a certain amount of xenophobia built into our brains from our suspicious prehistoric ancestors, and sometimes that primitive part of our minds will mistake "unfamiliar" psychic vibrations for "disturbing," and then equate "disturbing" with "wrong" or "evil." A better choice would be to *(a)* observe from a respectful distance, *(b)* record in your journal what you've seen, if you wish, or even make sketches or take photos, and *(c)* look for someone who might have more familiarity with the culture in question. Be careful who you choose to ask. "Satanic Panic" is an awful thing. Finding a symbol is not the same thing as finding a dead human body. (If you find a body, please call the police.)

make the ethical choice

If you are reasonably sure that some magical or religious group is actively doing something that you consider truly harmful, you have a variety of ethical choices. You can do nothing. This is perhaps safest. You can do a spell to bring justice/karma to them, although please remember that it will also rebound upon you. This might be a good or bad thing. Don't dish out what you can't handle getting back.

Another possibility is doing a binding spell for the specific behavior that you can't abide. This will have one absolute side effect: You will also be prevented from evidencing this behavior, with other possible effects as well. First, it might bind your fate and energy to theirs. Second, it might bind you from doing some other behavior that is as unethical as theirs, and as difficult for you to stop. The gods are like that. Third, if you're mistaken and they aren't really doing anything of the sort, it will bounce back in rather uncomfortable ways. So be very, very careful before you take on the role of Magical Vigilante. It can backfire.

don't assume you're cursed

Don't assume that everything bad that happens to you is the result of somebody's curse. Even if you don't believe in past lives and whatever karma is held over from them, you are not snow-white pristine, you have made mistakes, and anyway, sometimes Shit Just Happens.

The ancient Greeks believed that there were two kinds of Fate. The first, *ananke*, was also known as *moera*, which comes from the old word for a house lot. Ananke was your "lot." Bad stuff happened randomly, and you were there. It's not personal. Some fifty people had to get hit by that flood, and your house was there. Some percentage of children were going to be born blind this year, and yours was among them.

The other kind of Fate, called *heimarmene*, was the stuff that happened to you because of choices you had made in the past. Sometimes it had happened so long ago, and took so long for the consequences of your actions to come around again, that it felt like ananke, seeming to come out of nowhere. There was an entire cult, the *Kynikos* or "Dogs of the Goddess," whose entire philosophy was based around sorting out your ananke from your heimarmene. From them, we get the modern word "cynic."

The upshot of all this is that when something bad happens to you, the last thing you should assume is that someone is out there trying to curse you. First of all, if you've done the things you should with regard to the chapters on defenses and purification, it will not be easy to curse you anyway. Second, you are not that important. Look to your own life and choices first. If worst comes to worst, it may be just a bad bump in your road. We all have these, and some are worse than others. It's okay to do spells to help you get through a hard time, but try everything else before you fixate on deliberately inflicted curses from the outside.

think outside your tradition

Do take the time to politely read up on other traditions. This includes asking people in the know. Sometimes they will be very helpful, and eager to share their knowledge with you. Sometimes they won't want to tell you anything, due to secrecy, fear of disrespect, or you being the wrong sort of person in their minds. Don't take it personally. Retreat politely, and try somewhere else.

For example, if you want to learn about Santería, banging on the doors of all your Hispanic neighbors is not a good idea. First, don't assume they are anything but garden-variety Catholics. Second, they are under no obligation to tell you anything. Your best bet is someone giving a public talk on that subject, and your second-best bet will probably be a botanica (Afro/Cuban/Caribbean spiritualist shop).

It's good to learn about other traditions, especially those around your neighborhood, even if you don't intend to practice them. If nothing else, it will give you information on how not to step on people's cultural toes. You can also learn a lot by watching; keep a journal and be your own occult field researcher. Things that are not clear now may become clear later. If you actually find someone who is glad to talk to you, ask them first thing about what customs to keep in mind with regard to sacred and ritual space.

Then there's always the library. Do try to get at least two sources with the same information (and make sure one isn't just quoting the other) before believing anything.

think before you speak

Terminology can be tricky. For example, the word "witch" is being reclaimed by the Neopagan movement, but to most indigenous and transplanted Paleopagan religions, their only meaning for the term was inherited from Christian missionaries and conquistadors. These admittedly biased folks informed them that the word "witch" was to be equated with whatever word in their tongue symbolized a magic-worker whose magic was outside that accepted by the village, and usually harmful. When they hear you call yourself a witch, that's what they might think. It's unlikely that they will accept your definition that it has something to do with some ancient European tradition that they may never have heard of.

Some alternatives might be to say that you're a "spiritualist," or interested in spiritualism (which does not, to them, have the same meaning that it does to Madame Blavatsky and the table-tapping Victorians); that you work "good magic" or "white magic" (they might not believe you, but at least you're trying); or you can say that you are a "goddess worshipper" and see if they are interested in more information.

When dealing with people of Native American descent who live and worship in the traditional ways, never, never call yourself a "medicine man" or "medicine woman." Be careful with the word "shaman" when dealing with them, if you can; although it is an old European word, those Native folk who have heard of it might know that most white people equate it with "medicine person," and may feel you are taking on a title you have no right to. You can argue with them about it if you want, as it is technically a white people's word, referring to a Siberian Chukchi spiritual worker—Raven has done so in the past—but if harmonious interaction is your goal, you might want to avoid it.

Such words as "medicine man/woman," "shaman," "curandero," "bruja," "houngan," and so forth, have cultural expectations attached to the title. If you do not live up to these cultural expectations—and it's unlikely that you can, unless you know a lot about the culture in question, in which case you know not to do this anyway—you will be looked at as a liar or an idiot. Don't even try it. You can make comparisons if you are very, very careful and there is no language barrier. If they can only get one word out of three, there will probably be misunderstandings.

By the same token, don't use your words to describe them, except with extreme caution. Even the word "pagan" may mean, to them, an uneducated and ignorant hick, which was its original meaning as communicated by the aforementioned Christian missionaries. They may not appreciate being labeled as such—e.g., "You're a Pagan too, like me!"

respect sacred space

Be especially respectful of the sacred space arranged in people's living spaces, be it your roommate's altar or shrines set up in a house you're visiting. This goes not only for people of other religions, but for other Pagans and magical practitioners as well. It is always acceptable to ask, when you first enter someone else's home, whether there are particular places that you should not touch, go near, set your drink down on, and so forth.

When you are sharing an apartment with other magical practitioners, be clear in delineating private and public space. Keep your altar and magical implements in your room, and if there is something that absolutely cannot be touched, don't take it out in public rooms. Before setting up any kind of a house altar, do a lot of negotiation as to what is going to go on it. Each symbolic item has to be acceptable to everyone in the house, and also to every deity represented. Don't put feuding deities' items next to each other. Decide in advance what the goal will be for this altar, whether spells for the house will be done on it, or whether it will be strictly worship. One household did regular spells together on theirs for food, money, sex, and other useful items; another household made theirs a turning-of-the-year altar and only seasonal worship items were put on it. If you can't agree on how to do a spell for the household, you can all do the spell separately in your own rooms, preferably at the same time.

If you are going to hold a ritual in your house, especially if there are going to be a bunch of people coming in, please clear it beforehand with your housemates and be specific about when you will be coming and going, what will happen, and how much privacy you expect. This is especially important if the ritual will be done in a public room, or will be noisy. If you do solitary magical practices in your room, shield it well and learn to keep the energy focused and quiet. Your roommates don't need to get splashed with it as it goes by.

If you decide to do a house cleansing, not all of your roommates need to participate. However, you should be very courteous about going into their spaces. No matter how much of an emergency you think it is, if a roommate forbids you to enter his or her room, you shouldn't violate those wishes. You can create a shield to block off the energy and keep it in their room (draw a line across the threshold of the room with a finger dipped in a protective oil), or you can use a loud sound that will reverberate throughout the apartment when they aren't there.

In general, try to avoid feuds with your roommates. If disagreements do happen, do not succumb to the temptation to take it out on their magical space or tools. Dumping things on their altar or stashing poppets or lit candles in their room is not the way to go about things. If it has come to that point, perhaps you should be either evicting them or doing magic to find yourself a new home.

Multiculturalism is a wonderful thing, but sometimes it takes a lot of work. Some cultures are fairly isolationist, usually due to one of three reasons: (1) fear of attack, (2) fear of contamination, and (3) the idea that secrecy brings power. Privacy needs to be respected. Researchers need to be patient; the way Tannin slowly got information about Santería was to first become a customer in a botanica, and then gradually to forge a relationship with the owner, who was willing to share general information. Don't rush, don't push, be careful and respectful, and remember that all roads lead to the top of the mountain eventually, in their own way.

fourteen

In To the Depths

UNDERGROUND

• • Whenever you read a book that lists many different kinds of deities, they usually start with the gods of fertility who roam about on the Earth, or perhaps the bright sky gods, or the gods of sun and moon and star. They progress through warrior deities, gods of the arts and inspiration, gods of work, and other natural gods of the sea and rivers and animals. Finally, at the very end, they get to the underworld gods of death and darkness. Assuming they bother to mention them at all, that is. It is likely that the mention will be cursory and the tone almost a whisper, and that no spells or magics will be given in order to invoke them. After all, why would anyone want to? (At least, this is an attitude you may run across in some books and Pagan circles.)

And there are a few books who err too far in the other direction. They talk excitedly about the death gods as if they are some hot new rock-and-roll stars that it's cool to hang around with, and extol wearing black and dangling skull pendants. They mention death and rebirth without really going into what that all means, and they give the impression that clergy dedicated to these gods have little to do other than wear dark, tattered clothing and impressive jewelry, and intone long chants before smoky altars. This is just as insulting, in its own way.

Every culture has its own death gods, and although they are a varied bunch, they vary less, in many ways, than an equal group of multicultural fertility gods, or sea gods, or sky gods. Death, loss, and endings are universal. They are all implacable, and terrible. There was Hel, beautiful woman on one side and rotting corpse on the other, lady of snow and ice. There is dark, retiring Hades with his helm of invisibility, the God Who Wasn't There. The Afro-Caribbean Yorubas have Oya, the Storm Goddess and La Dueña de el Cemetario (lady of the cemetery). For the Babylonians, it was Ereshkigal, whose idea of a good date was to hang you on a meat hook above her throne.

Current majority religious culture tends to associate both death and darkness with evil, but the Pagan view is to see death as a natural, if painful, part of the life cycle, and darkness as the place of mystery and the unknown, from which comes all creation, and creativity. The deities of the dark are powerful and not to be trifled with or made light of, but they can be good friends in time of grief or darknesses of the soul.

In ancient times, priest/esses of the death deities had a number of very serious responsibilities. These included things like caring for the dying, preparing their bodies for burial, presiding over funerals, comforting the survivors, caring for the insane (who were thought to be temporary residents of the Underworld), and other not-very-glamorous tasks. Sometimes they were paid in the clothing of those who had died, which gave rise to the Irish *bean sidhe*, the wailing woman who washes the bloody clothes of those soon to perish.

Today, in the Yoruba faiths such as Santería, Voudoun, Candomble, and Umbanda, priests dedicated to Oya, Lady of Death and the Storm, La Dueña de el Cemetario; and Obatala, the giver of justice and compassion, split those duties between them. Followers of Obatala lay out and wash a corpse, organize the official mourning, and comfort the family. They bear the corpse to the cemetery to be buried, and once it is inside the cemetery it belongs to Oya. Her followers are also in charge of making sure the dead stay dead, laying ghosts and battling necromancers.

In cities, the most common place for people to die is in hospitals. In fact, hospitals are the reason so many people who don't live in cities end up dying in them. The number of ghosts in a particular hospital will vary, depending on the practices of that hospital. The constant cleaning and antiseptic treatment that the average hospital gets is actually a good way to clean out negative energy residue—including ghosts—but it also cleans out positive energy residue, which is why hospitals feel sterile as well as smell that way.

However, the way most of us experience the Underworld is not through our own deaths (at least not at first!), but through times in our lives that are dark and difficult, or through inner battles with our own dark sides. This can feel very much like death, a death of the soul, even though our bodies still live and walk around. This is just as legitimate an experience of the Underworld as is communing with ghosts, and much more accessible, even inevitable, to the average person. Usually, when we are trapped Down There, there is something that we need to find before we can come up. In all the legends—Orpheus, Inanna, Persephone—there is something that we must do or contact, and the best and quickest way to find it is to ask the management. The Dark Goddess and Lord of the Dead, in all their forms, are usually willing to help, as long as you don't expect their help to be particularly gentle or respectful of your feelings and delusions.

The places in the city that are most conducive to this kind of depth work are the underground areas. Not every city has subways, although the biggest ones do, but nearly all of them have sewer systems that are accessible by manholes (we do not advise entering the sewer system bodily, as it is highly dangerous and probably illegal). Whether or not you want to take the risk of going down one is your business, but if there is a subway system you can access, use it.

There is power under the ground. Ancient cultures frequently had their sacred places in caves or crypts under the earth, from the Hopi kivas to the "incubus" holes. One reason is that the deeper down you go, the more exposed you are to ley lines. These are the lines of energy that run through the Earth's crust like a web (see chapter 17, Migration). Tunnels can be cut right through them, and the exposed and interrupted energy pours out through the narrow channels. It's why mentally disturbed people are drawn to living down there, aside from the protection, privacy, and lack of rent. If you stay down there too long, it can cause a certain amount of mental disturbance in its own right, but that's because it's too much sustained power for humans to stand in for long periods, not because it's bad. It's actually quite powerful, and useful for working magic.

Part of the reason that the subway is associated with death is not just the darkness and the underground area but the sense of motion, of being snatched away and taken down a tunnel at high speed with many others. In the motion of the subway you can see a metaphor for the angels of death, who are always coming and going, from one pickup to the next. There is also the fact that the subway is labyrinthine, and the labyrinth has long been a symbol of the Underworld, and one's own twisted depths.

Meet Your Monster

Making friends with one's own depths is an important thing. Everyone has monsters living inside us; it's part of being human. Some of those monsters are cruel, and some are petty, and some are terrified and weak and sniveling. Some are versions of our frustrated inner two-year-old, who wants it all NOW; some were born from painful and traumatic experiences. Some of them are unsafe and can't be allowed to make physical decisions, and some are just mortifyingly embarrassing. We lock them in cages in our psychic basements, and usually we pretend that they aren't there.

However, the longer they're kept in the dark and are never allowed to get their needs met, the more twisted they become, and the more they begin to plot sabotage of the rational minds above. We are confident that they are completely under control, perhaps even that they don't exist any more, and then suddenly we fall in love with someone totally inappropriate, or blow up at work, or develop ulcers or cancer, and we can just barely hear their muffled "Ha! Gotcha!" from the basement.

After years of work with the Darkness Within and Without (and by dark we do not mean evil, just terrifying and mysterious), we've come to the conclusion that the best way to deal with the denizens of your inner Underworld is by the following steps:

1. *Accept that you have monsters, and that they will likely remain monsters, and try to scrape up some kind of affection for them. If they don't feel loved and cared about in spite of their grubbiness, they get worse. Treat them with the respect due to wounded veterans suffering from post-traumatic stress disorder.*
2. *Show that affection by giving them little gifts. Obviously, you can't give in to all their atrocious demands; you'd end up dead or in jail. But you can find small things to do that give them pleasure that don't harm others. We've found that monsters demand way too much when they think they aren't going to get anything, and when they start getting some attention they scale back their demands. (An example of this might be: If your monster is filled with rage, cast a circle in an empty backyard and smash a whole bunch of bottles. Please clean up after your monster, however.)*
3. *Build them a nice park to play in, inside yourself. Give them toys. Make sure there's a strong wall around the park, if need be, but make it pretty inside. Bring in friends for them to play with—perhaps other people's monsters, under carefully controlled and negotiated circumstances. An example of solo monster coddling might be putting up things your monster likes to look at on the walls, or dancing to music that your monster likes. An example*

of mutual monster coddling might be role-playing your monsters together in an agreed-upon manner, or sharing a mutual but unusual hobby.

4 *Don't try to force them to heal, or get better, or un-monster. That never works. It's the equivalent of beating an angry child to force them to be happy. Maybe they'll get better with lots of unconditional love and attention, and maybe they won't. Either way, it's better than having them sawing holes in the floor beneath you.*

The underground, which symbolizes the Underworld, otherworld, land of the dead, and cave of the depths, is the place to leave messages for your monsters. If you eventually intend to bring them out into the light, you can leave messages for them in subway trash cans. The trash eventually gets removed and taken up above ground to a dump where it is recycled, burned, and so on. If they have to stay in your metaphorical basement because they're too dangerous to run your body or make decisions for your life, toss the message on the subway tracks or tuck it in a crack somewhere.

Offerings for the Dark Deities

If you're depressed and feel as though you're trapped in an underworld of despair, a good deity to call on is Persephone, who traveled to the underworld and eventually became its queen, but only when she accepted its dark king, Hades, as her destiny. She cares for the dead and everyone trapped down there, and is very compassionate. If you can get a pomegranate from the store, dedicate it to her and eat it, asking her for help. Go down into the subway and leave six of its seeds for her, and she will respond. Sometimes this response will be to send a Mercury/Hermes figure to be your guide out, which could be someone like a therapist, or someone who travels a lot, or an intellectual who has read a lot. It might even be a book rather than a person, or it might be a ticket to somewhere else.

blood

You can create small altars and offerings to the Dark Ones, if you're discreet. In Boston, the subway is built so that you can sneak a ways around the corner and leave items in the small alcoves created by the support beams. Traditionally, in almost every culture, the Death Gods are given offerings of flesh and blood, preferably as raw as possible. If you don't keep meat on hand in the fridge, go to the butcher shop and get some. Even a sprinkling of blood from the butcher shop will do. If you're female and between the ages of puberty and menopause, you have a fresh supply of blood every month that you can offer them; put some on a cloth and wrap it up. If you really want to get their attention, you can cut yourself slightly with a sharp knife or razor blade (we suggest an X-acto blade) and shed a few drops of blood into a cloth, being careful to sterilize the knife and your skin so as to minimize infection. Please don't do any cutting while in a dirty subway; do it at home in a clean room and bring the cloth down afterward. Since any kind of blood is a safety hazard for other people, if you've shed more than a couple of spots—say the knife cuts a little deep and you spill more than you expected—an acceptable way to handle it is to microwave the cloth afterward to sterilize it, or even to burn it to ashes and scatter them underground. Keep in mind that a little of your own blood as an offering is fine. Excess is not only unnecessary, but dangerous. If you do not value it, why should the gods?

Warning: The use of any kind of blood in Pagan ritual or magic is a controversial one in the Pagan community. The vast majority of beginning magic books advise against such workings, for reasons both of physical safety and public relations. The reason we have chosen to include guidelines for such workings is that we know that some people will choose to do them anyway, and it is better to have parameters for safety and appropriate context, rather than demonizing such workings to the point where someone gets hurt out of ignorance. As far as we are concerned, the only human blood that it is assuredly ethical to shed is your own.

candles

Use black candles. Some people associate them with evildoings, but that's a matter of intent, not color. (Speaking of which: Despite what you might think, the death gods are not amused by petty vengeance, and they do not suffer fools at all. They see time and karma differently than you do, with a longer view, and if you ask them for something they feel is frivolous, they will do nothing. Make sure the request warrants their intervention, since when they intervene, it will be extreme, for you as well as everyone else involved.) Good oils to use for annointings of self or offerings are cypress, musk, sandalwood, hollyberry, and clary sage.

Spells to Release

A good spell to release a person from your life who has died or left is to take a piece of newspaper or other soft paper, write their name on it, and descend to the subway. As you wait for the train, cut it up with scissors or tear it up, and as the train passes, throw the confetti pieces toward it. You need to time it so the gust of wind sucks the pieces away. Make sure, however, that you are ready to let go, or it will be ripped away from you whether you really want it or not.

You can also use this as a method for letting go of something else, such as an addiction or obsession, by writing the name of what you need to lose on a piece of paper, tearing it up, and throwing it after the train. The best trains to do this with are, of course, the ones that are just passing through and aren't stopping. If you only have trains that stop, wait until it is starting again, and be at the end of the platform so that it will rush past you, gaining speed. Some people like to visualize a great dark angel with spread wings rushing toward them.

Please be discreet, however; the authorities don't like you to litter. A small piece of paper works as well as a large one, and rush hour may not be the best time to do this sort of spell. Use your judgment.

Getting Underground

If you live in a city that has no subways, the symbolic underground is more difficult to get to, but not impossible. The kivas of the Southwest Native Americans had a small hole in the floor, leading downward, too small for a human to climb down. It was called the *sipapu*, and was the doorway through which the spirits of the ancestors could climb up, and offerings could be thrown down. Your city has hundreds of sipapus, all over the streets. We call them manholes and storm drains. While it is unsafe (and in some places illegal) to move manhole covers, they all have very small holes in the center that can receive such things as we list below. Storm drains are larger, and will take bigger items.

In the interest of not creating pollution or clogging problems, please be careful what you give for offerings. Anything you give the spirits of the underworld via the sewer system should be biodegradable. Offerings of food or drink are fine; wrappers are not. Small scrolls of paper (preferably unbleached, like from a brown paper bag), written with your request in words or symbols, is the most popular option. Message-shapes can be scratched into a shard of natural earthenware (not polymer) clay, or molded out of bread dough. Making the offering during a rainstorm guarantees that your wish will be carried swiftly to its destination.

Another area sacred to the gods of the underground is the city garbage dump. Some are off limits, and some aren't; if you can legally get into the dump, it's a good place to make offerings of things that you want to get rid of. It's a tradition around here that people doing the "I Quit" spell to break themselves of an addictive substance will go to the dump and get rid of their paraphernalia, or some symbol of their addiction. Anything placed into a landfill will go back to the land, eventually, but please take care and be safe: make sure that it's acceptable for you to be there, and don't crawl into any big machinery. Also, make sure that it's a real dump. In cities, trash piles often spring up spontaneously in empty lots or on roadsides. Don't contribute to this kind of littering.

Similar to dumps, recycling centers are good places to commune with the gods of death and regeneration. However, the caveat is that if you drop something off for magical purposes, make sure that you bring something back with you, to use or fix or add to an art project. Giving the Dark Goddess your pain is all very well and good, but try to lighten her load in return. If you can find anything at all at the dump that you might want to take back with you, do it, although most landfills don't have much that is safe to take.

Also, please make sure that whatever you drop off is actually something the recycling center will recycle; you can, for example, stuff your message into a used can or bottle. For that matter, a quick-and-dirty alternative to this is to write your message on a can or bottle and stick it into the recycling machines in many grocery stores. If you want to add an extra karmic punch, donate the money you get from the can to the charity of your choice. C'mon, how convenient is that?

fifteen

Ghosts & Ancestors

HANDLING THE DEAD

• • If you don't believe in ghosts, skip this chapter.

Still with us? Good. Just as there are more live people in the city, there are more dead people as well. This body count is added to by the fact that many people outside the city will die in the urban hospitals they are rushed to, and the generally higher rate of violence in the city. So cities in general will have more ghosts hanging around, and thus those people who are more "sensitive" will have to deal with them.

In this chapter, we will be working on several assumptions. If you don't agree with them, fine. However, we've developed these assumptions from years of observation on how things work, and we have to trust our own perceptions.

We are assuming that all human beings have something nonphysical that is usually referred to as a spirit or soul, and that it does not die with the body, but goes on, either to another body (reincarnation), another place (the underworld, land of the dead, summerland, and so on), hangs around this plane on its own (ghosts), or goes somewhere we can't even imagine. It is our personal opinion that any of these things can happen, and that each person's fate is unique.

Contacting Spirits

Contacting spirits that have already departed is the most common form of necromancy. It is also asking for trouble. As someone who is sworn to the death gods and has a close relationship with the Dark Goddess and the Lord of the Dead, Raven would like to point out that they do not approve of their charges being messed with by the selfish breathing folk. It's one thing to gently and respectfully attempt to contact one soul; it's something else entirely to walk into graveyards and bother them for no good reason. And, frankly, there *is* no good reason. In fact if, as we assume, there are lots of places for a dead soul to go, they may not even be around to answer. They may be a preschooler in Chicago or Beijing by now.

There's also the issue that contacting dead spirits is a process fraught with difficulty. Most of the common methods available can easily be hijacked by spirits, benevolent and not-so-benevolent, and by the subconscious wishes of the person doing the contacting, or the medium. The most infamous of these methods is the Ouija board.

We'd like to put in our personal two cents about these items. First of all, it makes no difference as to whether they're made by Hasbro or made from a piece of paper and a shot glass; they'll work either way, if the right energy connection is made. Second, in our opinion, to use one is to ask for trouble. It doesn't matter if they're decorated with angels or blood-dripping Gothic lettering. To use one is to call a pay phone in space, to pick up the cosmic line and dial one and any ten numbers, with the added inconvenience that the anonymous being you've contacted might even be able to crawl back along the line and come into your living room. The "entities" that you contact might be nice or nasty; they might be toying with you or lying or just plain crazy. If anyone tells you that astral entities don't lie or attempt to mess with you, they're full of it. And you will have no way of knowing what you've got on the other end. There's also the fact that it's very easy for one's subconscious to move the planchette by itself, telling you what you want to hear. Very few humans are disciplined enough not to move the planchette by themselves. An insistent "No way, man, I didn't move it!" does not constitute sufficient proof.

Talking to the dead, in the first place, isn't very useful or fun. Contrary to popular belief, the dead do not all know about each other. They do not know all the wisdom of the universe. They do not know where all other souls have gone. They cannot tell you the Secret Name of God. There's little point in bothering them.

Some spells, and some cultures and traditions, will have you doing magical work in a cemetery. Examples of such rites might be rituals aimed at reverence of the ancestors, and remembering the beloved dead. In Oriental custom, and in certain Southern communities, picnics and celebrations in graveyards are common. Be respectful when you enter a graveyard, even though not all the spirits of the people buried there are actually present. Actually, only a few of them may be there, but for those few, this is their home and should be treated as such. If you have to take something or perform something, leave an offering and apologize openly to any lingering spirits before you begin.

Some cities will have their own cemeteries, especially older ones like Boston or New York. However, in newer cities, the dead are banished to outlying areas or their yards are fenced and closed up. There is, however, the city morgue.

The single exception to the general "don't-call-on-the-dead" rule is your own ancestors, especially your close relatives. The urge to reproduce and see our genes prosper is a basic human urge in all of us, even those of us who have voluntarily sterilized ourselves. Like all the great survival instincts, it can last beyond the grave. Family is family, and if you really must call on the dead for help, call on those dead who have the greatest vested interest, in the long term, in seeing you surviving successfully. If the family members you've actually met, such as your parents and grandparents, aren't people you'd call on for the time of day if they were alive, you may want to go further back and propitiate ancestors who died before your birth—as long as you aren't asking them to work against actual living relatives who are bothering you. Do the research to make offerings to them of things they would have liked in their time, and make offerings of those things. You might want to read aloud to them from their religious book, even if it is not what you personally practice.

Ancestor Altars

It's a nice thing to set up an altar for your ancestors in your home. This can work especially well with children, giving them a chance to know something about the people whose blood runs in their veins, who died before they were born. Such altars are usually very discreet, little more than a collection of photos and old heirlooms, with a white candle. By making offerings to them periodically, you thank them for your body, the gift they have bequeathed to you. You don't have to have every ancestor present; if you didn't get along with one of them, it's best not to encourage their spirit to visit.

Ancestor altars are common in many cultures. The Japanese create special niches with scrolls and photos; Afro-Caribbean folks use photos, candles, and *egunguns* (short sticks with streamers of cloth attached to them, usually cut from the deceased's clothing or clothing that they would have liked). Jewish tradition sets out small white candles encased in glass called *yortzite* candles, with or without photos, on the anniversary of the loved one's death.

Ghosts

What we call "ghosts" are spirits who, for whatever reason, have not moved on and are attempting to stay on this plane. The most common reason is simply a refusal to believe that they are dead. These ghosts wander about, still stuck in their routines, in a state of denial that can go on for centuries. Traumatic, violent deaths may create such shock in the person that they are not rational enough, at their time of death, to accept it. Other ghosts may feel that there's something important they need to do that their death interrupted, but this might be something as trivial as getting the (long dead) sheep back into the pen before the (long dead) wolves show up.

Whatever the reason, ghosts don't last long. If they're exceptionally strong, they can last for a few centuries, but they slowly fade away unless there's some source of energy there to feed them. When ghosts are drawn to us warm, living human beings, it's usually to try to get some energy off of us in order to sustain their "life." The strong emotions that they cause in us will do the trick, unfortunately. When ghosts start to really wreak havoc on the living, it's usually to get fed and sustained.

hauntings

The most common form of ghosts and "ghost sightings" is the haunt, which is not the same as a single-entity ghost. A haunt is a kind of psychic imprint. Something traumatic and horrible happens to someone, causing them to emit a terribly strong burst of emotion and psychic energy, and possibly (but not always) causing their death. It then becomes like a kind of looped psychic tape, playing and replaying, triggered by the presence of fresh energy, such as a breathing person wandering through. They manifest as cold spots; sounds; sudden brief, flashing hallucinations; and strong, alien emotions coursing through one's body. They are quite common in such places as dormitories, hospitals, mental institutions, and hotels, especially if the place is old enough that a lot has happened there.

The materials used to build the place make a difference as to whether or not a haunt will "stick." Plastic does not absorb well, and neither does glass or fiberglass. Stone and concrete take a lot of energy to imprint, but they can hold it for a long time. Metal also holds well, as does wood or bone, which was once alive and had its own energy.

Haunts respond better and easier to cleansing than do ghosts, but the cleansing must be thorough and probably repeated. Burning a bit of smudge does not work. The first step should probably be an actual physical cleaning, preferably with strong chemicals such as bleach or ammonia. If the problem is extreme, rooms may have to be renovated. Taking down the walls and replacing them with new material may help; even a coat of paint will help. Then you can go about smudging, incensing, and doing general banishing/cleansing. (See chapter 4, Internal Hygiene.)

actual ghosts

Actual ghosts are rarer then they are claimed to be. Most sightings of ghosts and spirits aren't. Period. But for the occasional *real* unquiet spirit, there are several methods to use to deal with them.

If the ghost is in your house, you will have to decide whether or not you can coexist in the same house with it. Some ghosts are fairly harmless, and even entertaining; others are not. You may find it amusing or even comforting to have one around, or you may want your house to yourself and feel about the ghost the way you would about a squatting prior tenant.

The first step is to attempt to make contact with the spirit. You'll want to find out what area the ghost is manifesting the most from. If the pipes bang, check the basement. Yes, it can be in daytime and the lights can be on. (For what it's worth, light doesn't bother a ghost. It simply distracts the human eye and mind from glimpsing it, and thus makes us feel safer.) Then you might want to light some incense to attract them, such as sweetgrass or dittany of Crete. Talk to the ghost out loud, even if you can't see, hear, or sense it—not everyone is a medium. Be firm, but polite. Ask it politely to leave or, if you've decided that it can stay, tell it that you'd rather it didn't mess with your things, terrify your family, or levitate your pets. Ask it to behave. Say that you want to communicate with it, although you may not be able to hear or understand it. If you're sure that it has to go, tell it that it is dead, that its time has come, and that it will be happier on the other side of the gate. If need be, light a black candle and ask the gods of the dead to come and collect it.

Most spirits will respond fairly well to this treatment, receding to the background or leaving as asked. The minority that are a problem—the ones that like to scare you, send you hallucinations, move your things around, and so forth—are probably fading out, hungry for energy, and willing to get it any way they can. For them, banishment is in order.

banishments

First, let's talk about the different kinds of banishments. When you read books of magic, especially ceremonial texts, you might come across the words "Greater Banishing Ritual" and "Lesser Banishing Ritual." Different groups have different wording and versions. They will vary in complexity and strength; sometimes the LBR is a solitary work and the GBR is a group activity. Generally speaking, however, the LBR disperses the energy of the spirit, disrupting it enough so that it dislodges, and the GBR locks it out completely or destroys it. One option is to use one of these. We suggest that you contact ceremonialists who know how to utilize them for advice.

On the other end—kitchen folk magic being on the opposite side of the spectrum from ceremonial magic—there is an old folk charm that suggests a way to get rid of spirits. Cook a dinner, using all the best dishes, set an extra place for the spirit, serve it the food, and eat dinner yourself. After you've finished, open the front door, and tell it that you have fed it and now it has to leave. Dig a hole and bury the food afterwards, returning it to the earth. If you live in a place where it's not safe to dig in the ground, you can give it to someone who needs it (like a hungry street person) in their honor.

Another option, especially for nonviolent spirits, is to do several cleansings and purifications over a period of days or weeks. (See chapter 4, Internal Hygiene.) However, if you've tried all these things and nothing is working, don't go it alone. Call in a whole lot of friends to help you out and do the banishing ritual of your choice; there are plenty to be found in books. Be careful what people you invite; this is not an opportunity for a keg party. You need serious, centered, strong-willed magical practitioners who are not going to freak out or become hysterical or joke around.

Ghosts are, in general, nothing to be afraid of. Although we've been scared by a few, we've never found any actual evidence of someone who was killed by one. We humans like to scare each other with tales of haunts and horror, but the delicious thrill we get from retelling that ghostly hitchhiker myth for the twenty-ninth time actually detracts from our ability to calmly and effectively handle an actual haunting when it occurs. If you think you've got a ghost problem, spend a lot of time doing calming breathing exercises. The more sane you are about dealing with it, the less it can harm you.

sixteen

Spirit in the Wires

MAGIC OVER THE MODEM

• • Even as we speak, the online community grows by leaps and bounds. Even as we write, hundreds more people will haltingly find their way onto the Internet . . . and some of them will be Pagans. It's likely, though not true across the board, that they will be urban Pagans. In her second edition of *Drawing Down the Moon*, Margot Adler addresses the fact that a disproportionate number of Pagans work with computers. Their reasons varied from "computers, like magic, rely on symbolic and patterned thinking" to "computers are where oddballs are often employed" to "Paganism is a right-brained change from left-brained computer work." Whatever it is, the online Pagan community is growing by leaps and bounds right along with everything else. It's been a boon to those solitaries who were the only witch in their town, and felt like the only witch in the world. Suddenly there's a hundred, a thousand, five thousand people to talk to with whom they have something in common. It's been a boon to people not in a coven who need support, for Pagan clergy who need new ideas for their rituals, for confused beginners who need guides through a morass of often-conflicting book information. It gets folks together for events and protests, gets out the local and national news about us, and generates lively (and sometimes overly intense) discussion about who we are and what we believe.

Granted, it's a rather classist community. In order to join, you have to have a computer with the right software and a modem. You have to have a phone line that it's okay to tie up for periods of time. You have to have an ISP, and although there are more and more free ones, the most reliable ones still cost money. You have to have electricity, and that means an apartment with utilities. You have to have the free time to hunt around and find Pagan-oriented sites, lists, and newsgroups. There is still a whole strata of people who can't afford food and clothing, much less these luxuries, and you won't find them on the Internet, more's the pity.

However, for what it is, it's pretty good. We've met more Pagans over the 'Net than we ever did putting up a sign in the local bookshop, and although we've never seen most of their faces (except perhaps photos scanned into their websites), we have a definite friendship connection with them.

Rituals and Spells in Cyberspace

There are other kinds of connections, too. The first time we got onto Pagan lists, we noticed that there were periodic calls for online rituals. This boggled us—the idea that people could hold ritual in cyberspace, as it were, sitting thousands of miles away, and it could work!

Cyber-rituals seem to be done in one of two ways. Either everyone goes into a particular chat room together at a particular preselected time, and the ritual is typed in by the leader, or everyone does it in their own home at a particular time, blending their energies, and posts something specific onto the 'Net as the final act of the spell. The former kind seems to be the most popular, allowing folks who live many states away to perform ritual together like a coven. Indeed, there are many online covens, made up of individuals who may never have seen each other in the flesh, but who do workings together. Those we've spoken to admit that it is harder and takes more practice to raise a group cone of power when the people involved are not physically present with each other, but also that it is neither impossible nor terribly difficult.

Cyber-spells are even simpler. Everyone agrees to do a specific thing, and then goes off and does it. It's almost like pooling the combined energies of a whole group of scattered solitaries. The system can be as simple as sending out an email to a list of people you know, asking them to focus some positive energy your way for a particular goal, or it can be far more complex.

One email list that we know of has an official "basket keeper." This person has a magically blessed basket on her altar, and whenever anyone needs something magical, they email her and ask her to add a snippet of ribbon to the basket, of a particular color that reflects their need. When several people are working on the same spell, they each send her an email asking her to add a ribbon for each of them, putting the ribbons in as a group but naming each of them separately as she does it. Another group has timed rituals—they send out the spell, or poem, or specific act that people are supposed to do or concentrate on, and list the times, in each time zone, that it should be performed, so that everyone is in synchrony with each other.

> "I live in a pretty conservative town, and I currently live with my devoutly Christian parents and my two kids. While I work two jobs and attempt to make enough money to get us our own place, I have neither the time, the energy, or the unfettered atmosphere to roam around searching for other Pagans, drive miles to circles, find babysitting, and explain to my parents why I'm wearing a robe and smelling of incense. At night

on the 'Net, though, I can be part of an online coven, I can do spells with the witches on my email loop, and no one in our house has to know. And it's relatively cheap. Without my online Pagan community, I'd be completely isolated."

ANONYMOUS KENTUCKY WITCH

Cybershaman

One of the terms that we've run across many times on the 'Net is the word "cybershaman." It's a slippery term, just now finding its legs, and it seems to mean different things to different people. We took a survey across the Internet, asking certain people how they would define this ambiguous title, and the responses were many and varied. Some folks called themselves cybershamans in order to communicate that they were Pagans with 'Net access, or Pagans who sold things over the 'Net, or did readings over the 'Net. Others went a little further and claimed to do healings and other spells through the modem-to-modem interface. Some, like Ernie Vega (quoted below), sold special magic items such as magical screen savers, or virtual Internet Tarot cards, or some other product specifically designed for use in magical work.

"Technology has provided tools and methodologies that allow for devices to aid in the creation, accumulation, and direction of energies. These devices range from quartz crystal-based arrays and Radionics devices to computer software that utilizes the computer's ability to create virtual environments with the aid of ancient geometrical formulas and Kabalistic and other numerical systems. Symbols are another means of focusing and accumulating energy. When an object or symbol is focused on, it absorbs and takes on the nature of the directed focus. This has been shown to explain many religious as well as magical phenomena. When directed focus is used in combination with symbols, the result is a system that allows a trained practitioner to manipulate energy without the investment of significant personal energy depletion. . . . A Cybershaman is an individual that possesses the required combination of skills and hardware that can be used in unison to practice Psionics."

Ernie Vega, http://www.gocs1.com

Internet "Magic"

Although there is a lot of magic going on with regard to the Internet, there is also a lot of fakery as well. Recently a bunch of folks in a chat room got all anxious when a .gif (picture icon) appeared "magically" in the middle of the chat room at an auspicious moment, and they couldn't figure out where it came from. Discussions went on in the cyber version of hushed whispers, conjecturing as to whether it was the manifestation of a spirit. What we have to say about such things is to remember the quote: "A sufficiently advanced technology is indistinguishable from magic." In other words, just because you can't figure out where it was slipped in doesn't mean it was supernaturally inserted. Anything that "appears magically" was most likely to have been put there by someone with fingers and a keyboard, who is probably at this moment laughing at the furor he caused.

This is a sister syndrome to the one that has people certain that everything that goes wrong in their lives is the product of a curse. We all want to see wonders and know mysteries, but most things are really a lot more straightforward than you'd think. Occam's razor still applies.

That said, there is a certain school of thought that feels that the Internet itself has grown in energy to the point that it has begun to develop its own soul. Thousands of people are tuned in to it at any given time, and that is a lot of focused human energy. People have reported feeling as if the 'Net was "aware" and observing them. Whether or not this is the case would probably be the work of a whole other book, one which we might spend the next ten years cheerfully researching. We may not be able to cover the entire subject in this one chapter, but we should point one thing out: Just because something is developing soul and awareness does not mean that it will think like you. You needn't blame emails that go astray or jumbled files or wandering viruses on a sentient Internet. Most likely it would manifest in a completely different way. Keep in mind Captain Kirk's quote: "What does God want with a spaceship?" and look at things with a grain of salt. Sometimes a little skepticism lends a nice, tangy flavor to your sense of wonder.

> "Sometimes I'll just go into a trance while 'Netsurfing, and that's when the gods speak to me. I'll click and click and click, going from one link to another without really reading the pages, just clicking on the first link I see on each page, until suddenly some Power yells 'Stop!' and I look at where I am. It might be something I need to know, or learn, or a personal message of some kind. It might also be someone who needs something I have to give, perhaps some work or knowledge, and I've been sent to their site in order to give them some important thing. Figuring out which it is, that's the fun part. But I've met and helped a lot of people this way, surprisingly, and they've helped me too. When I can tune out my own thoughts of the process and just let the intuition roll, that's when it happens. That's when I'm on duty."
>
> *Spider, self-proclaimed cybershaman*

Resources

We'd wanted to give a listing of Pagan resources on the Internet, but the problem is that the Internet changes so quickly, from month to month, that half of what we put down might well be obsolete by the time this book gets to the shelves. Instead, we've decided to list Pagan resources that have been around a while and don't seem to be vanishing any time soon. (We also recommend the book *The Wiccan Web* by Patricia Telesco and Sirona Knight, put out by Citadel Press.)

If you want to find an online coven, we suggest starting with the following sites, especially The Witches' Voice, which has state-by-state listings of Pagan contacts. We also suggest that you get onto an email list site (such as Yahoogroups or Topica), run the word "Pagan" through their search engine, and join a group. Every online coven that we know screens its members heavily; unlike a face-to-face coven where you can gauge someone's behavior, tone of voice, body language, and general energy, email gives you only a bunch of printed words on the screen to work with. Most online covens prefer to invite people themselves, on their own time. Contribute to a Pagan email list that interests you—and there are many, many lists to contribute to—and make it known casually that you are interested in joining an online coven, and wait to see if anyone invites you. If all else fails, start one yourself.

the witches' voice

http://www.witchvox.com. Probably the best resource out there for the seeker. Has lasted seven years thus far, and shows no signs of disappearing, so it's probably safe to list here. An enormous site, it may take a bit of surfing around to find all of its information.

the covenant of the goddess

http://www.cog.org. Been around for a decade. COG is one of the oldest and most respected legal Pagan churches in the country. Their regular polling tries to estimate the total numbers of Pagandom. Do bother to take their polls, when they are up.

america online

Chats such as Ask A Witch, Ask About Witchcraft, Pagan Crossroads, Pagan Tea House, The Circle, or Virtual Magick. Message boards such as Pagan Chatter, Pagan Groups, or Pagan Fellowship. To find them, go to the AOL People Connection: **http://aolsvc.cc.aol. com/ peopleconnection/** and run them through the search engine.

yahoogroups

www.groups.yahoo.com. Sign in, get an official password, and type "Pagan" into the search engine. Hundreds of lists will come up. Read through them and decide which sound most useful to you. Some are screened and some are very open.

May the sacred touch of Grandmother Spider
And the Weaver of the Fates
Protect me from harm
And the machine that is the horse I ride
Protect from all ills
As I crawl across this great and marvelous Web.

PROTECTIVE CYBER PRAYER

Download your Dagdafiles

Download your Dagdafiles
For I hold the PGP key to the Gates of Horn
I am the Path
And the Server
And the Host
The Lurker in the Sharewarewood Forest
And the Sysop of Internettingham
I am the Troll under the Rainbow Bridge
The Access and the Offramp
I am the Yule Login
The ELM and the PINE and the APPLE
First in the Printer Queue
And the Passwyrd to Arcadia Online.
Yea, for I am the Screen Savior,
The reboot of the Biosphere.
I am a hard drive of seven sectors.
I have been a zipfile before all.

I have ReLeyed down the Landlines
Danced the Calling Circles—
Yea, I have harrowed dev.null
And been Uplinked again
I have been Crossposted,
I am the FAQ
And the Sword in the Spam,
The Account
And the Pathway
And the Drive Internal;
I am the Expansion Card,
I am plugged into the MotherBoard,
I am a Window on the C,
I am a .Wav of the C,
I am a Soundblaster of the C.
I have Crashed
And gone down in Flames
I have Doubleclicked the Bucket
And been Recovered.

MagicRat, 1995

seventeen

Migration

MOVING ON

• • Most city dwellers move a lot, at least a lot more than rural folk. This is partly because most city folk rent rather than own their homes, and also partly because due to the small sizes of living areas in the city, people tend to think of their home as the space created by their stuff, and not the space created by their building. Buildings are interchangeable, assuming the basics of location, utilities, neighbors, space, amenities, cleanliness, and aesthetics are acceptable.

Tannin's grandmother told her, when she was young, that you should always leave the toilet brush when you go. Buy a new one if necessary, but the toilet brush stays. She wasn't too specific, but Tannin got the idea that it had to do with leaving in an emotional space of generosity, of wishing well to the next tenant, in accruing good karma that will then be turned around on you. Not to mention the act of leaving your shit behind. Tannin laughed at it, but found herself leaving the toilet brush anyway—for sanitary reasons, she told herself. Then, when she was poorest, moving into a place with hardly two cents to rub together, she discovered that this time she didn't have to buy a new toilet brush—the former tenant had left theirs.

Her relief was more than just not having to spend two dollars on a new brush; it was more than that. It told her that the universe keeps score in a good way, not just with your transgressions; that what goes around really does come around. Now she tells everyone who moves to leave the toilet brush. You won't be disappointed, we promise.

Movin' Out

On moving day, after you move everything out, go around the place and sweep with a broom. Do this even if the whole place is carpeted. As you work, imagine that you are sweeping out all of your energy and memories, leaving the place clean for the next person. If you live in a group apartment with other roommates who are not moving out, do your room and any common areas that you may have utilized, such as the kitchen or living area. If you parked on the couch a lot to watch TV, sweep the couch. If you sat on the front porch to watch folks walking by or play guitar, sweep that area as well.

If you're moving because you were lovers with someone in that particular apartment, and you've just broken up, it would behoove you to sweep out their room as well, if possible, to remove your energy from it. This is assuming they will let you in. If they won't, there's an alternative method of emergency energy removal through closed doors that you can use.

Stand facing the closed door, and press your hands against it. Close your eyes and visualize the traces of your energy, like little glittering traces that only you can see, scattered about the room beyond the door. See them in the curve of the bed where you might have climbed in, on the chair where you might have sat, on the rug where your footsteps fell. Inhale deeply, filling your lungs, and imagine you are sucking these particles out. Close your mouth and exhale through your nose. Repeat, seeing your traces fade in your mind's eye, until it feels like you've done enough. Then walk outside, face away from the building, take a deep breath, and exhale hard, blowing all that away. It helps if there's a high wind that you can blow it into.

If your belongings need to go into a storage facility—for example, if you're temporarily homeless and sleeping on people's couches until you find the right apartment—make sure that you do a quick protection spell inside the storage area before you close it up and go away. We made a small mojo bag and hung it inside from an upended chair at the very top of the pile. You can also make a small offering of crumbs or cheese to the rodent spirits, and ask them to leave your cubicle alone. Leave the offering just outside the lot, not inside it. Similarly, if you are driving a moving truck across the country, put a safety spell in the interior to prevent breakage.

Home-finding Magic

Of course, the most important part of moving is having the right place to move to. Some people are lucky; they know exactly where they are going, have plenty of time to move, and plenty of money to do it with. Some people aren't as lucky. Home-finding magic is useful and important; you never know when you'll find yourself in a spot where you need to find a new place, fast.

You could turn to our chapter on the Triple Urban Goddess and implore Squat to help; have a marathon dirty joke party with your friends in her honor. Or, if you work with Yoruba deities, you could make an offering to Yemaya, Mother Orisha, of white wine and blue corn chips. Or, if you prefer traditional European deities, talk to Hestia, lady of the hearth. Hestia needs to be invoked with fire; even a candle is a start, although a hibachi or small fire lit in a wok is even better. If nothing else, you can talk to the pilot light in a gas stove or furnace. No, really; those are Hestia's messengers.

Another way to do it is to make a fantasy map of the home that you want. Things can be in scale or not; you can show the lot plan or just the room grid if it's an apartment you're looking for. Draw or paste in any interesting features you'd like to see. Magazine picture collages are good for this. Anoint it with oil, and then hang it on your wall so you can look at it each night during your house-hunting period.

Still another method is to ask the city spirit to help. Find the "heart" of your city; go to the place where your city god lives. Bring an offering—a full bottle of beer, rum, a nice roll, or a bar of chocolate; whatever you think your city would appreciate. Sit under the statue, on the steps, or as close as you can get to that nexus where your city's spirit is most manifest, and close your eyes. When you are prepared, address your city respectfully, out loud or silently. Say to it (him or her) that you have come to ask a favor in a time of need. Explain that you want to remain within its domain, but have lost or are about to lose your housing. Tell it that you are willing to do what it takes to find a new place to live but that you need guidance and help. Offer your gift, and thank it for its time. Then start searching!

Here's an example of a prayer that Tannin has used in the past with good results:

"O Worcester, I have lived within your limits for over a half a decade. I want to stay here, and remain your subject. Unfortunately the apartment situation I am living in is falling apart. No one is happy. My roommates quarrel bitterly with one another and with me. Two of them have stolen money intended for bills and rent from the rest of us. My cats and I will need a new place to live very shortly. I cannot afford to live alone, or to pay significantly more for rent and utilities. I need to be able to get to work safely and surely so that I may pay for my living expenses. Please help us find a new place to live. If anyone that knows me needs a roommate, may that person or people come forward! If there is an advertisement that fits my situation, may I come across it in my search! Thank you for listening to my plea, and I hope you will accept this offering of bread."

If and when you do find housing, return to the site of your offering and thank your city for its help.

When the Entire Tribe Is On The Move, things can get chaotic. A whole household is more difficult to find housing for, but not impossible. In the year's time that this book was completed, rent control was lifted in our state. While this meant that landlords could increase revenues, which could be used to renovate their properties and increase their values, it also meant that a lot of our friends found themselves unable to keep their homes when it came to renegotiate their leases. Rent on one "inexpensive" four-bedroom apartment jumped from about $1200 to $1900, not including utilities such as gas or electricity. As a result, five people and three cats found themselves having to make other living arrangements within ninety days.

There can be many other reasons that a group of urban tribespeople may suddenly find themselves on the move. A big ol' yellow sticker across the front entrance of the building emblazoned with the legend "CONDEMNED" might be one. Another might be finding oneself saddled with dangerous neighbors. In the case of some people Tannin knew, they decided to move after one of their roommates was awakened by a glassy-eyed "guest" of the next-door neighbor tripping over the frame of his futon after jimmying their living room window open with a large knife. When Tannin's stocky, heavily tattooed, dreadlocked friend confronted the intruder with a bellow, he mumbled that he had lost his keys and scrambled back out the window. City dwellers might suddenly find themselves unable to meet the conditions of their lease, like an associate who lived in a "no children" complex and found himself having to find housing fast upon coming home one day to find his ex-wife with their children on his doorstep, begging him to take full custody of the kids so that she could go into drug rehab. The possibilities are endless.

Finding an apartment for a group with special needs (wheelchair access, pet-friendly, child-safe, and so on) can be a real bear to deal with. People in such a situation often find themselves in heavy competition for the limited housing that suits those needs.

ritual for securing housing

The ritual that follows is for an entire household of people who have a place in mind but aren't sure that they can get it.

Gather together:

1. *A short stake of wood (can be an old table or chair leg) around 1 to 2 feet long*
2. *Craft supplies such as markers, paint, string, yarn, carving knife, glue, and so on*
3. *Strips of cloth from the clothing of every person in the household who is moving*
4. *If there are pets, get discarded bits of fur or feathers from them (possibly gravel from the bottom of an aquarium tank for fish)*

Cast a circle or create sacred space the way you normally would. Everyone should be present. If you light candles, stick to the colors of red, yellow, white, or brown. Everyone should concentrate and visualize the whole tribe happily living in the apartment or house.

Then pass the spike of wood around the circle and decorate it. Give it a head and face. Its expression should be wide awake and watchful. Each member of the household should dress the spike in a strip of cloth from their clothing. While they are attaching it, they should say something like, "I hereby lay claim on the house on Number 43 Such-and-Such Street." They can also lay claim on some aspect of the house, such as, "I claim the bathroom first thing every morning!" When the stake is complete, lay it in the center of the room and everyone should join hands around it. Chant, sing, dance, make noises, or do whatever it is that you do to raise power, and then together raise the stake and fill it with that power, saying, "This place will be ours!" Then wrap it in clean black or white cloth, and sometime in the next twenty-four hours go together on a "scouting party" and hide the object carefully on the grounds of the house or apartment.

ask the house

If you find a place that you like, and aren't sure if you're going to get in—perhaps the landlord is considering someone else, or you have bad credit, or you won't give up your two dogs—there is one small method of recourse, especially if it's an old building with a "personality" all its own. Go to the building itself—after dark if you're embarrassed to do it in public—and talk to it. Tell it that you'd like very much to live there, that you'll take care of your living space and have a lot of fun in it, that you'll bring pleasing and happy vibes for it to enjoy. Ask it to see what it can do about arranging things so that you can live there. Then, even if you don't get the lease or mortgage immediately, keep checking back. The building could be working on it. After all, buildings are more like rocks or trees than like people or animals; their perception of time is very different, and it may take them some time to get it done. It may suddenly be open one day when you're checking in.

feng shui

If you're into learning about it, you can check out each new place by Feng Shui rules. As a complete oversimplification, Feng Shui is the Chinese art of figuring out whether or not a particular building is sited and proportioned to be magically fortuitous. Some people swear by it, including Raven's wife, who boggled realtor after realtor by doing strange measurements with a little chart at the front door of each house they looked at while house-hunting. She would check her charts and her compass, and then make such pronouncements as "Fertility! Good!" or "Might let in demons! Bad!" For what it's worth, the house she did finally approve has served them well for three years now.

From what we can discern, about half the Feng Shui rules are actually based on ways to deal with the geographical features or cultural quirks of its native China. For instance, houses facing certain directions are unlucky largely because that is the direction that weather comes in from the Yellow River, and houses at the end of dead-end streets are bad because medieval Chinese fire departments had a hard time getting to them in the event of a blaze. One would suppose that new rules would have to be invented for each geographical area of the world. In some cities, entire neighborhoods might be marked as having bad Feng Shui . . . muggers and drug dealers can't be all that fortuitous.

However, if you don't feel ready to learn all the traditional Feng Shui rules, you can use an abbreviated European Pagan version that Raven refers to as "Not Feng Shui." Just bring a compass and look at the four directions. Rooms in the eastern part of the dwelling would theoretically be good for starting to face the day, facing morning, and so on. Having a bedroom there would be great if you were trying to train yourself to get up early, though not so good if you work third shift. Kitchens and breakfast nooks—anywhere you eat the first meal of the day—would be most fortuitous if located in the east, as would study areas because of the east's association with the mind.

Rooms in the southern area would give the most energy—again, possibly not the best place for a bedroom, unless your sex life is sluggish and you want to wake it up. Spending time in a southern room might keep you up late nights—Raven's computer room is on the southern exposure, and it's where he spends most of his 3 A.M. awake time. The west would be the best place for a bedroom, with its association with romance and emotional peace, and also bathrooms. One would assume that there might be less plumbing problems and general trouble with the Water spirits in a western room. The north would be a good place for family gatherings, late-day meals, possibly the kitchen, rooms for winding down in the evening, and any workshops where handcrafts are done or things are made by hand.

However, even if every room in the house is in the wrong place, you can still manage by calling traces of the more appropriate elements into it. Bedroom in the south and you'd rather it was in the west? Bring water into the room with a fish tank, or sea-colored curtains over the bright southern-exposure windows. Keep getting distracted in your western kitchen and want more grounded Earth energy in it? Paint the walls green, or bring in plants along the western wall. If a particular room feels cramped to you, because of small size or odd shape, and the energy can't pass around it freely, hang mirrors on the wall that you wish was expanded outward, and it will increase the energy flow.

ley lines

Another issue when choosing a home is that of ley lines. These are the lines of energy that run under and through the ground everywhere. They're even present in the city; urban development does not eliminate them, although concrete does muffle them and they are better felt underground. (See chapter 14, Into the Depths.) Ley lines can be as thin as a garden hose or as wide as a road. They come in two varieties, positive and negative. This doesn't mean good or bad—more like A/C and D/C, or yin and yang. Positive ley lines give off energy and aren't good to have running directly under your bedroom. Negative ley lines absorb energy and aren't good to have under any room except your bathroom. Underground water generally follows negative ley lines, and water likes that energy and will carry any excess away with it. A ley cross, or the place where two ley lines cross over each other, is extra-strength voltage. A negative ley cross would be great to build a compost heap on, but not so good to live on. A positive ley cross can feel good for a while, but will give you headaches after long-term exposure. A ley cross composed of one positive and one negative line would be great for a place of power to do magic work, and is the only one even remotely safe to live over.

The other problem is that the energy of ley lines can be intensified by severe landscaping, like the kind contractors do that involves leveling hills and filling in small valleys with heavy equipment. Normally, ley lines are underground, and you feel the energy vibrating up from them, but if the earth is cut away to the point where the raw center of a ley line is exposed—and worse still, a house is then put on top of it—it can cause illness in the people living on and around it. This is most likely to be a problem in new housing developments where there has been recent massive digging just before home erection. If you check out one of these and feel vaguely uncomfortable, nauseous, or headachey just from walking around it, an exposed ley line might be the culprit. Don't move in.

Dowsing for ley lines could be a book in itself, so we won't go into it in detail here. However, if you don't have a knack for it (and neither of us do) or don't want to learn it, there are professional dowsers about who will gladly trot their Y-rods out and check a site for you, and they will know what you're talking about when you ask them to check for ley lines.

One method a friend uses for choosing an apartment is to bring her Tarot deck, walk into the main room of the possible dwelling, shuffle the deck, and lay three cards on the floor. Clearly, the Five of Pentacles would imply that the rent is going up astronomically quite soon, the Tower might imply a serious need of repairs, and if you pull the Ten of Swords you should probably leave in a hurry. On the other hand, the Ten of Cups or Pentacles would be a much better omen.

roommates

Once you've got the place and moved in, do a house cleansing (the one in our Internal Hygiene chapter works well) and set up your protective spells. The next thing to think about is who you're going to be sharing this place with. In the city, more people who are virtual strangers live in close proximity to each other—having housemates is simply cheaper and more cost-effective for lower-income people. The final spell in this chapter is one to attract the right kind of roommate. First, make a list of all the traits you want in a roommate. Don't forget to mention the lack of negative traits; for example, "Doesn't smoke," or "Doesn't have a lot of emotional baggage about cleaning," and so on. Make two copies of this list.

Now put one on the kitchen refrigerator with a magnet. Anoint it with a sweet-smelling oil or something else that'll smell good. One person we know rubbed freshly baked bread on it, in order to attract a roommate who would become a comfortable and homey friend. Take the other copy, fold it into a paper airplane, and release it into the wind somewhere—perhaps off the top of a high building, or out the car window on the highway. Then place your ad or ask around, and the universe will make sure the right individual comes along.

eighteen

Wildlife Identification

URBAN TOTEMS

• • The city is inhabited by thousands of tiny life-forms, many of whom we despise, but each of which has a simple power all their own. Those urban magicians who spend their lives in concrete jungles often have totems very different from the ones we are used to from looking at traditional rural animal "medicines"; although you will find Bear and Wolf and Eagle in the streets, their powers are alien there. They do not move through the city with the ease of Rat or Pigeon or Cockroach, and the city's secrets are not their expertise.

There is no creature of nature hated by the gods. All have their uses and value, and all hold secrets of survival in the difficult terrain of the urban jungle that human survivors would do well to respect and emulate. Learn what knowledge the urban totems have to give, and you make yourself stronger.

Just a terminology primer: There is a difference between the terms *totem animal*, *power animal*, and *familiar spirit*. A totem animal is symbolic of the spirit of the entire species; having Rat for a totem, for example, means that you have a two-way affinity with the entire rat species. You feel kinship with them, feel bound to protect them, and they teach you ways of being in the world. A power animal is similar in that it is also the overarching spirit of a species, but it is one that comes into your life to teach you something. Power animals can be temporary, until you have learned a specific lesson. Familiar animal spirits, on the other hand, are specific animals, often deceased former pets. A familiar spirit is almost like an animal bodhisattva who stays behind in order to help a specific person.

Common Urban Totems

rat

Rat is an often-despised animal in Western folklore, but rat is the first animal of the Chinese zodiac, associated with industry and good fortune. The Hindu God of Good Fortune, Ganesh, rides a rat, and rats can be found everywhere in ancient statuary, from a perch on the Buddha's hand to the bases of Cernunnos statues. In India, the rat is sacred to Sri Karniji, and hers is a temple where rats are tended and allowed to roam freely, believed to have a healing power by that goddess's good graces. Rat was endeared to the old Craft as the counselor and familiar of prisoners, possibly derived from the old belief that a small animal was the form a soul might take upon leaving the body of the deceased.

Rat is the undercover agent of the gods; he can be found everywhere in the world, from fields to subways. His life is a mystery to most; a lurking presence peering from the shadows or shuffling by, counting on his mystique to keep humans out of his way. Confrontation is not in his nature, but when battle is joined, no quarter is asked or given; like the proverbial cornered rat, this small creature has teeth. Rat, like the human animal, has no overwhelming survival advantage, and relies on cleverness and strategy to survive. He has a sardonic wit and keen senses; as an outsider, he often has a cutting remark, or at least thought, about almost any folly. Known in the East as the "Destroyer of Obstacles," he can bring down a mighty structure from the inside, finding and showing the weak points by gaining an inside perspective. Rat is the quintessential scavenger; he lives on things and in places that other creatures will not have; he lives off their excesses, trusting Lady Skor to provide . . . if one man's trash is another man's treasure, Rat can be quite wealthy indeed.

Rat totem people are difficult to spot; it is not a totem many seek, or often acknowledge. They are jacks-of-all-trades, and if they

W. Michael (Wolfie) Dooley

rat

are master of any, it is survival. Keen senses and general dexterity seem to be traits common to Rat people. Their vigilance, however, can turn to paranoia and solitude; even the most confident will prefer to keep a back to a wall and an escape route in reach at all times. As Rat is associated with bringing plagues and disease, Rat people must take care not to become carriers of some of the toxic influences among which they walk. Do those purifications! Rat folk thrive on things that most others would consider unhealthy; a Big Mac eaten on the move may be their soul food, and they gain sustenance from parts of the city that most people find blighted and benighted. Their sacred offering spaces are gutters and basements and storm drains and subway tunnels, places where Rat's domain intersects with the urban waking consciousness. They can often dig up forgotten things and find uses for scraps of lore . . . and learn a great deal about people from what they throw away.

cockroach

"Alms for the brown and six-legged!" Cockroach is the totem of endurance. Kill her by the dozens, by the hundreds, and she returns by the thousands. Shower her home with poisons and she breeds children who are resistant to them. It is said that in the event of a nuclear war, the cockroach may be the only survivor. Her power lies in her ability to evolve quickly, to turn mass death into improvement, to endure anything. She and Rat vie for the position of being King and Queen of the City, any city.

Cockroach is also probably the most reviled of all the totem animals, and the most hated. She is feared as a sign of filth, even though no diseases pass between humans and her kind; she is hunted and killed everywhere and welcome nowhere; she haunts us with fears of death, although she cannot harm us. Still, cockroaches curl up together in the walls of many, many houses, a social creature who cuddles with others of her kind, rarely fights, and carries her babies snugly on her back until they are old enough to turn white

cockroach

as adolescents and take their places. Cockroach is the ultimate pariah and, as such, her power can be called on by those groups who are seen as pariahs, cast out and reviled for sins they have not committed, whose only chance is simply to endure in secret until their enemies have moved on.

Cockroach people are quick, quiet, long-suffering, and keep a low profile. Often they are members of some minority group that is highly discriminated against, and Cockroach people must live daily with suspicion, hatred, and fear of sudden violence. They endure abuse and unfairness without complaint, shrugging it off, and go back about what work they are allowed to do. Like their totem, they may freeze suddenly if threatened, only moving their invisible antennae to take in the atmosphere and a possible escape route. Often they move with a hunched-over scuttle, as if afraid of retribution from above. They are good scavengers, taking what they can get and making do, and are good parents if poor disciplinarians. They move into a job, a neighborhood, a city, a relationship slowly, discreetly, almost as if they hope you won't notice until it's too late; and they are loyal friends, although they are prone to low self-esteem and need lots of reassurance. Cockroach totem people become bold only when they are in a group; the morale of the mob gives them courage to act. They are usually undervalued for their skills and patience; don't make the mistake of overlooking them. They may eventually inherit the Earth.

W. Michael (Wolfie) Dooley

mouse

Mouse totem is quiet courage and quiet industry. She works constantly, finding useful things to line her nest, bringing in more food and resources, shyly peeking from her corner hole to assess the safety of an area and prepare to make a run for it. Mouse is brave, because she must be. Her survival depends on it. She runs fast and keeps to the shadowed corners, but she never considers not going out because it would be too dangerous. She knows that the crumbs have to get from the kitchen floor to her children's bellies, never mind the schemes of marauding cats. She quickly figures out the best way to be unobtrusive and unnoticed, and does what has to be done.

The city can be a frightening and dangerous place, especially for people in less than ideal neighborhoods who are less than strong. Mouse totem is the one to call on when crossing those dark alleyways; she will teach you how to wrap yourself in a cloak of you-don't-see-me and pass unscathed. Mouse magic is about invisibility.

Mouse people are shy and quiet, often so shy that you don't know how brave they really are until they run out and pull the child off the subway tracks. They move quickly, scurrying from place to place, always busy. Home is especially important to Mouse folk, and their homes are often havens of domestic comfort and simple luxury, like hidden oases in the tumultuous urban jungle. They are very particular who they allow into those safe havens; a Mouse totem person won't invite you home after the first date, and probably won't go to your house either. A quiet but public restaurant is safer. When you make it over the threshold, you've earned their trust. Mouse folk are beloved of Squat and can always find that perfect cozy little apartment that just opened up when they need it. They are always a little uncomfortable out in large, open places or noisy crowds, and prefer to do their jobs in back rooms or kitchens and then go home, sliding safely through the dark streets in their mantle of inner safe space.

raccoon

raccoon

Raccoon totem is an opportunist. He is full of cheek and mischief. If you try to harm him, he runs away and laughs . . . but not before stealing something of yours. He can be kind and generous, but he can also take advantage of you wickedly. He will make those around him look like fools, but when things are turned around on him and cause him to look like a fool, he handles it gracefully . . . after the laughing stops. His fits of fury at the moment make him all the funnier. He protects the fool and the troublemaker, but will not extend his protection to the malicious.

Raccoon totem people, like the Coyote folk, often flirt with the law—rarely in violent ways, but only in small misdemeanors. All too often, the small mischiefs that they deem harmless are seen quite differently by those in authority, and they end up in court. Unfortunately, Raccoon people are not big on discipline, and these are the charmers who screw up their probation or anger their guards without meaning to. They need to use a little judgment to make sure that their zest for living does not wreck their life. They live to party and have a good time, and the drudgery of a full-time job wears on them. Ideally, they should have an unusual profession that allows them to use their comedic timing and natural talent for being a "character," such as a radio DJ or a club MC. They can be surprisingly loyal to a mate that they love, and who will put up with their erratic trickster nature. They are good with other people's children, although somewhat at a loss with their own, as they aren't used to being authority figures and don't adapt well to the self-sacrificing nature of a parent-child relationship.

W. MICHAEL (WOLFIE) DOOLEY

robin

robin

Robin is beauty in strength. He dominates the field, keeps the best food for himself, and the other birds do not look on him with fondness but with grudging respect, not only because of his strength but because of his simple beauty. With his coat of soft grey and red breast, Robin is also the harbinger of spring, and he stays through the summer. He is a companion of the Sun God, and his sky-blue eggs, also solar symbols, have been the delight of children for many generations. He protects and lends strength to bullied children and other victims of the city's social dynamic, aiding them in rising above the victim mentality.

Robin totem people are the ones who rise above their backgrounds and traumas to become successful in whatever they do. They are the ghetto mothers who manage to feed eight children, get them through high school, and keep them out of gangs. They are also the boss that everyone likes, but who is still definitely the boss; the one who demands your best work but will let you off without a murmur when the children are sick. Family ties are important to them, but only the family members that treat them with respect, or that they are able to help rise in the world. They like to mentor people and help them improve themselves, if they deem you worthy of it. Robin feels that everyone should take responsibility for their own situation, and is not likely to approve of political schemes that give less qualified but more oppressed people an advantage. Robin types are often physically impressive specimens with a handsomeness that is not so much exotic or gorgeous as wholesomely pretty, putting you in mind of fine trees or the smell of a bakery. They exude a firm, strong, solar warmth.

W. Michael (Wolfie) Dooley

starling

starling

Starling totem is strength in numbers. Starling is the fierceness of a community protecting itself. If a larger bird tries to attack a starling on the fringes of the flock, the whole flock will attack him and drive him off. Starling is plucky and proud out of proportion to his size, because he knows that he can rely on his neighbors to protect him, and that he will protect those who need it in his own turn. Starling guides and protects those fighting, as a community, against governmental oppression or encroachment of the unwanted into the community.

Starling totem people are feisty and loud. They are gossips who care, the community watch member with the binoculars who watches through the window (and sometimes into your house, but only to make sure you're okay, of course), and the little old lady in tennis shoes who shrieks in rage when her neighbor is burglarized, and ends up picketing the mayor's office with a crowd of cronies. They will bring you a full meal when you're sick and then stay for an hour to give you advice on how to get better, whether you need it or not. They do tend to get carried away rather quickly with a cause, especially one that allows them to feel righteous indignation; but it is often the fierceness of Starling totem people that gets politicians' attention when more diplomatic types are ignored. And with a troupe of Starling folk at your back, you can change minds and make a difference.

SEAN PETRIN

squirrel

squirrel

Squirrel totem is resourcefulness. Squirrel is small, but he knows how to use his teeth, his claws, and his speed to his advantage. He knows when to flee a fight and when to stand his ground, and he can be vicious. Squirrel knows the value of setting aside useful things for the future, of knowing his environment and using it to his advantage. Squirrel guides one to the resources, within and without, that one needs to survive. Squirrel is the foreteller of a bad winter; he knows instinctively when bad times are coming and begins to stockpile for them.

Squirrel totem people have whatever strange item you need in their basements, or they have the phone number of someone who does. They can spot a bargain a mile off and squeeze a penny so hard it squeaks. Squirrel people are beloved of Skor. They are cheerful gossips, especially over buying/selling/trading discussions. Squirrel folk tend to chatter when nervous, and squawk in incoherence when angry. They are ingenious with tools and oddments—when you lose your keys in the mall, it's the Squirrel totem friend who will hot-wire your car for you with a paper clip and a ballpoint pen. If you're in luck, your mechanic will be Squirrel totem and save you money by the dozens of junkyards he's got a line on, chock-full of interesting items for the scrounging. They are bright-eyed hard workers. You can always tell a Squirrel house by the amount of junk stored in it, often in random piles that no one but Squirrel could ever find anything in.

kitty

kitty

Kitty, the domestic cat, is the beloved of luxury. She is sensuous and demanding, affectionate and selfish. She'll brighten your day by curling up in your lap, purring, just when you've had a bad time, and the next day dig her claws into your leg because you bought an inferior brand of cat food. She is utterly certain that she will be taken care of completely, because she feels she deserves it. Her self-confidence is supreme and she rules the roost with a combination of cajoling charm and arrogance. She is the patron of those who seek luxury for its own sake, who long to roll on satin sheets and be served fine food on delicate dishes. She is the love of beautiful things, but she is afraid of the streets and knows, instinctively, that she is out of her league there. There is still a streak of the killer in her nature, however, and she will use it when those she perceives as vermin intrude on her harmonious situation.

Kitty totem people almost always grew up either affluent-to-wealthy or the pet of the family, perhaps an only child. They generally got what they wanted with charm, and it was generally available to be given to them. They are all at least a little spoiled; if there was too much pressure in their early lives they would have turned toward the Feral Cat totem. Kitties can be either sex; all it takes is at least some money and privilege. They are at their best in a job where charm counts, but submissiveness doesn't, and where they can leave the day-to-day nastiness of survival to someone else to take care of.

feral cat

feral cat

The Feral Cat began as a wild thing, became a domesticated creature, and returned to the wild again. He has a special bond with humanity, but it is an uneasy bond, full of suspicion on both sides. He will readily accept the gifts of man, but his lifestyle—whether chosen by himself or by fate—is his own, and he will make the best of it. He is ultimately incompatible with the softness of houses and canned food, which he leaves to his domesticated cousin, Kitty. The Feral Cat is protector and companion to the spiritually and the physically homeless.

Feral Cat people are hard to get close to. When confronted, they either shy and bolt, or slash out at you verbally and then run. They do not trust easily; they have often been victimized in the past, but they cultivate a chip on the shoulder as a better alternative to a helplessness complex. It takes time and work to get past their barriers of mistrust, and although they may eventually become loyal friends, they will never completely give up their freedom to leave. Their killer streak is even more pronounced than that of Kitty, and they make vengeful enemies who hold grudges. They often have a wild, compelling beauty that inspires others to do all sorts of ridiculous things in order to win them, and they are notorious for leaving a long trail of broken hearts.

SEAN PETRIN

pigeon

pigeon

Pigeon totem is protection in numbers. Unlike Starling, Pigeon is passive in his conflicts; while a whole flock of starlings will attack an infringing intruder, pigeons will scatter in all directions, on the theory that the intruder can catch only one—or may not catch any—in the ensuing confusion. Pigeon is clever and witty, and watches the city go by in all its wild and lively glory with quiet humor. He knows how to sidestep trouble; he is the anonymity of the crowd. Pigeon is the protector and companion of those who thrive in the city by simply going with the flow, laughing at frustrations, and enjoying the thriving life and rich culture to be found there.

Just as there are a lot of pigeons in the city, there are a lot of Pigeon totem people, happily living lives of moderate comfort, bustling about and doing their business frugally and carefully. They are not ambitious; working in a bookstore until the age of eighty is just fine with them, as long as they have a decent wage and a warm family life. Actual pigeons shelter their young under bridges and overpasses until they are old enough to face the world and its dangers; that's why you never actually see any baby pigeons. Like their totem, Pigeon parents may be fairly overprotective, or at least very invested, believing that their children are having a sheltered, happy childhood. They may want their children to go to private school, less out of hope for their prospects than for worry over their safety. Pigeon totem children may consciously or unconsciously expect such overprotective treatment, and may not do well in families where they are expected to be more independent or decisive while still young. While Starling may be more of an activist, Pigeon rules social clubs—the local Scout leaders and the heads of the Elks' Club and Ladies' Auxiliary are probably Pigeons, gathering their friends about them for clucking, chirping, and mutual aid.

W. Michael (Wolfie) Dooley

crow

crow

Crow is the long view and the messenger. Like Starling, Crow is loud and aggressive and finds strength in numbers, but unlike them, Crow is disciplined. Crow plans, oversees, organizes, researches. Crows post scouts, work in ordered gangs, and keep each other in line. No one's eyes are sharper or minds are keener; Crow doesn't miss a trick. He isn't afraid of death or carnage; he eats carrion and thus uses and recycles what others throw away. As such, Crow is the patron of those who routinely and dispassionately deal with garbage, whether human or inanimate. He has no patience with squeamishness or reticence; his preferred brand of humor is as black as his feathers. Crows may fight among each other with vigor, but when one of the sentries cries danger, they are together on the front lines. Sacred to the dark gods and goddesses such as Morrigan, Ereshkigal, and Valraven, they are the birds of omen used by death deities all over the world; to see one is to sit up and take notice. Serious things are coming.

The old rhyme regarding crows as a divinatory practice is as follows:

> One crow for bad news, two crows for mirth;
> Three for a wedding, four for a birth;
> Five for treasure, six for a thief;
> Seven a journey and eight is grief;
> Nine for a secret and ten for sorrow;
> Eleven reunion and twelve, joy tomorrow.

Crow totem people can always be known by their mouths when they get angry. Actual crows use insults as a dominance practice, and Crow totem folk are no different. Street Crow people know (and will use) obscenities that would make sailors blush, and more educated Crows can rip you to shreds verbally. Crow folk are fiercely loyal to their clan, and fairly amoral concerning anyone not in it. They can be found running family businesses, organizing political groups, and in leadership positions in groups that range from the

SEAN PETRIN

moth

Romany to the Mafia. Actual crows are notorious thieves, unable to resist anything shiny and bright and unwatched; occasional Crow folk may resort to stealing, although most will simply content themselves with snatching extra advantages, often without thought to the feelings of others. They have a harsh streak and need to work on developing compassion. Many are fascinated with death and work in a business concerning it, whether mortuary work, hospice care, suicide hotlines, or just ambulance chasing.

moth

Moth is the poet, the frail, delicate artist whose obsessions are her inspirations. She is drawn to the forbidden, the bright and dangerous, and risks her life in doing so, but it is from this dance of risk and desire that her muse grows and calls to her. Moth is the beauty of an ephemeral life, lived for today but with every ounce of energy in your being, which ends in a blaze of glory. She will sacrifice anything to achieve the experience that results in her art expanding and blossoming; she will expose herself to anything in order to learn still more and become still deeper, a fitting channel for whatever art she practices.

Moth people are brilliant, defiant, fragile, obsessive, and often self-destructive. They've done it all, mostly just for the thrill of it; if there's a drug they haven't tried or a decadent perversion they haven't sampled, it was probably boring anyway. They can live in garrets or squat in abandoned warehouses if it means the freedom to pursue their creative projects. Moth people often seem to resent the fact that they have bodies, and act as if they ought to be able to live on nectar and ambrosia. One Moth totem person bubbled dreamily about why she liked LSD; she was quite taken with the fact that she didn't feel a need to eat or sleep while tripping. "It's like being an immortal, living only on air!" she raptured. Moth totem people often attract admiring caretakers who understand that their charges are "special," and attend to regular meals and infected cuts and so forth. However, Moth folk are doomed to play the Flame Game, and too often self-destruct,

seagull

often burning their well-meaning caretakers in the process. The (slightly) more sensible Moths learn to listen—at least sometimes—to the people who love them, before they take themselves down in a torrent of excess.

seagull

Seagull is the rebel, unique and odd and proud of it. Seagull is an individual, and revels in his quirkiness; drawn to trouble, if there's something loud and dangerous happening, he wants to be in on it. Something of a tool-user among birds, he has learned to drop shellfish on hard rocks to break them open, and thus is the patron of those inventors who are trying to find a new, ingenious, and unexpected way to do things. Of course, this means that it is the seagull whom the sailors find most often tangled in their lines, mewing piteously, but when released he goes quickly back to his old ways. Like crow, seagull eats trash and can live on anything, and is often found in garbage dumps and in areas where there has been recent urban development—farmlands becoming strip malls, and subdivisions. Seagull has seen the wide ocean and, although he may be found surprisingly far inland, his heart is still part of the great swell and tide of the Ocean Mother. As a creature of Water as much as Air, he is emotional; his rebellion may be couched in terms of intellect, but its actual source is deeply felt emotions.

Seagull totem people not only make no effort to fit in, they like to rub it in the faces of more conservative types. They enjoy making people gasp and blanch, preferably as many as possible. The best of them are true activists, trying to change the world and working from their own unusual dreams. The worst are angry young men and women who rebel for the sake of rebellion, not caring who is trashed in the process or what the situation really looks like. Seagull people will say all sorts of untrue and hurtful things in the heat of the moment, and may later regret their words and say, "No, of course I didn't mean that!"—but by then they may have destroyed the trust of others, and their own reputations. They need to realize that their

W. Michael (Wolfie) Dooley

silverfish

actions stem from their feelings, and that feelings don't need to be justified but they do need to be considered before being turned into actions. Seagull people are creative, and always have a new way of looking at things; they can be a breath of fresh sea air in a maze of stuffy bureaucracy.

silverfish

Silverfish is the bookworm. She devours all things written on paper, and prefers to live among them as well. Quiet and unobtrusive, she knows that the best way to learn something from books is to immerse yourself in them. As an insect totem, she is a little removed from the hot, red-blooded passions of mammals and birds; she prefers precision and routine, and slow, delicate work.

Silverfish totem people are often researchers or librarians, or use some other excuse to spend their time happily buried in stacks of books. They know the public library inside and out, and will read about anything—it's the act of learning that counts to them, not the content itself. Print is sacred to them; it is the font of knowledge. They are reserved and find relationships based primarily on the heart or body difficult; to get to know a Silverfish person, you have to know enough, and have an interesting-enough mind, to make them feel like you're worth the effort of looking up from their book and paying attention. Many Silverfish types also love computers; they're the often-antisocial programmers who mumble a vague hello from their monitors as you walk in each morning, the remains of Szechuan food around them—they've been up all night, caught in the mysteries of programming, and you are nothing more than an annoyance to their train of thought. Indeed, many Silverfish totem people seem to live in a sort of trance, broken only by the intrusions of ordinary people. They are shy and need careful, intellectually stimulating drawing-out by people who won't be pushy. They do well on jobs that require deep thought and precise handling of details.

goldfish

goldfish

Goldfish is delight itself, swimming in her bowl happily, warming hearts and fascinating minds. She can range from the modest golden damsel of the classroom or day care center, or the gloriously extravagant Azumanishiki in the great tank at the local Japanese restaurant. Children love her and adults become children in her presence. She lives easily in a life bounded closely by glass, looking out but never attempting to leave. She is satisfied with her world and sees the happiness in it, finding meaning in what she has rather than what she might never achieve.

Goldfish totem people are optimists who are more concerned with beautifying their tiny corner of the world than in changing what they can't see, touch, or understand. They are often involved with children, and many teachers, especially on the elementary level, are Goldfish totem. They can see the delight in almost any situation; what kills them is darkness and having to breathe the foulness of emotional pollution. If the waters they swim in are thick with the anger, sorrow, or resentment of others, they will become sad and sluggish, and either become ill or leave. They manage to live fulfilled lives in situations that other types would chafe at as too restrictive; as long as their bowl is filled with sun, clean water to splash in, interesting objects, and lots of friends to frolic with, they're content. Goldfish totem folks have a need for beauty, although it need not be the luxury that Kitty prefers. They are the ones who always have potted plants on their doorstep, and buy flowers in the grocery store along with their food. Goldfish totem people live the bread-and-hyacinths adage instinctively. There is something childlike about them, even when they are old; they never lose their sense of wonder.

SEAN PETRIN

wasp

wasp

Wasp is fury on tiny wings. She works hard to build her nest in a safe place, only to have it destroyed; she cares ceaselessly for her many children, only to see them threatened by our encroachment; and she tries desperately to leave a room she has stumbled into, only to see us shriek and attack her. When she finally loses patience—of which, it must be said, she has little to begin with—and stings us, we fault her.

Wasp totem people are female, like Wasp herself. They have a very high level of energy, high standards, and a tongue of razor sharpness that they aren't afraid to use. They generally only attack when they or theirs are threatened, or when you get in their way, but when they do it's an all-out attack and you would do well to duck. On some level, conscious or otherwise, they feel that women are naturally superior, and this attitude often creeps out in their dealings with non-females and the females who defer to non-females. Most of the time, however, their wrath lies in abeyance and they busy themselves with buzzing about on their various projects. Wasp totems can get more done in a day than most of us get done in a month; they tear through daunting paperwork and manual labor with relentless efficiency. A Wasp woman's house is spit-and-polish; you could eat off her floor, although you wouldn't dare to try it. Her children don't have mismatched socks, and they get every speck of their homework done. A Wasp secretary is an asset to the boss and a terror to the rest of the office. Wasp is a social animal, and loves to join groups, although her favorite group activity is working on something useful with others, and she'll prefer to join clubs that have an actual purpose and track record. She needs to learn to loosen up a bit and slow down, enjoying the flowers instead of merely considering them one more job to do.

W. Michael (Wolfie) Dooley

dog

dog

Dog is loyalty and protection of territory. Dog can range from feral to domestic, like cat, but unlike cat he never fully becomes a wild creature. Dog has passed too far from his wild ancestors; feral dogs are not so much creatures that have become wild so much as formerly or potentially loving family pets who were abandoned, mistreated, or abused, and whose minds have broken into insanity. No matter how skinny and wild, in his heart of hearts Dog really just wants to be part of a family, a pack, a group he can serve and take care of, that will give him a feeling of belonging and affection. Dog is fiercely loyal, more so than any other totem; he will give his life willingly for those he belongs to. He has a strong sense of boundaries and territory, and even if he doesn't take it seriously (see that wagging tail!), he is compelled to bark a little at passersby just to make himself feel important and useful. Dog is a finder; if there's something to be turned up, he'll sniff it out. Call on Dog to watch your borders and call the alarm if anything threatens.

Dog totem people, once they trust you (and how quickly they trust you depends on how much they've been hurt in the past), will trust you forever and follow your word anywhere. They will be terribly hurt if you betray them and will either run away with their tail between their legs, never to return, or turn on you, snarling. Don't abuse their trust. Dog totem people are valuable allies and make good second- or third-in-commands. They may not have the vision and planning ability to be leaders, but they are superb at carrying out orders even in the midst of crisis. It's Dog who will do your detective legwork, patiently sniffing out details and uncovering truth. They are determined and don't mind repetitive work.

They are often the designated protectors of their family groups; often it's Dog who will own the weapons or the FID (firearms identification) card, just in case something should happen. Many serve their community by becoming policemen or other protectors. Dog folk have good internal alarm systems; when someone or something is sniffing around the boundaries, they know. Don't dismiss their

W. Michael (Wolfie) Dooley

sparrow

fears; there may be something to them not immediately visible at first glance. They will go into a howling rage the first time someone tosses a rock through their window, and if they don't own a weapon by then, they will quickly after that. When they are made angry, they see red and go for the throat, often not really considering the best plan of attack or whether they can realistically win; they need to be calmed down with soft strokes and made to think the consequences through before leaping to a possibly fatal defense.

sparrow

Sparrow is exuberance. He dances, he sings, he twitters his joy in living to the tops of skyscrapers. He is melodramatic and cheerful; to him, everything is larger than life. Sparrow's sorrows are cried to the rooftops and his joys sung on the sidewalks to passing strangers. He romances mates like no one else, showering them with affection and attention, risking his neck on wild flights of romantic fantasy, and missing that oncoming windshield by blind luck. Sparrow is lucky; it is what sustains him. He knows, on some level, that he can afford to be open and trusting to the universe, because it will take care of him; and if something goes wrong, well, it was all a great adventure anyway.

One example of the phenomenal Sparrow luck is that Sparrow totem people almost always reach old age, and reach it with their sparkle intact. They make the best sidewalk performers; indeed, they are the stagefolk who make you happy with their sheer infectious enthusiasm. They are supreme romantics all the way to the grave, and lavish their mates with affection and grand gestures. Happy is the mate of a Sparrow totem person who has the sense to close an eye to their occasional infidelities (they don't mean to do it, but the opportunity just arose and impulsively, they took it; it doesn't mean any more than just a grand experience) and can depend on themselves and others to provide for them. Sparrows are not good providers, unless their luck has directed them to a position where shrewd managers market their charm properly, and even then they're

SEAN PETRIN

ant

more likely to spend it themselves. They will take risks and gamble, just for the fun of it, and tend to be sucked into get-rich-quick schemes or taken in through their generous natures. Sparrow folk travel a lot and are often on the road, migrating from town to town in search of new horizons, new experiences, and new stories to tell.

ant

Ant is methodical patience. Order is her god, and any kind of disorder disturbs her to the point of temporary hysteria. She likes to have a place for everything, and everything in its place. Conformity is very important to ant, and in her nest she will kill anything that is not an ant. However, she is blind and rather gullible, and so other creatures may easily sneak in, disguised on the surface as ants, and so feast on her works and take advantage of her. While ant is the ultimate conformist, on rare occasions ant will suddenly grow wings and fly. The shock of coming into the unfamiliar medium of the high air after having existed only in her prosaic earthbound urban setting may mean her downfall, or it may inspire her to imaginative heights like she has never known before. A young queen ant may have her flight of fancy, and then upon returning to earth will wrench off her wings so as never to be able to fly again. However, her flight will have given her the inspiration to become queen of the other, less visionary ants, and they will slavishly follow her lead from then on.

Ant totem people are the most orderly on the face of the planet. To them, mess means danger; if the paper clips migrate from one side of the desk to the other, or out-things get put in the in-box, chaos might rule the universe. Everything they do is part of a huge magic spell to keep chaos from overtaking their lives. They are superb organizers, and can streamline a company in no time, but as a hive-minded insect, Ant people tend to see the whole as more important than any of the parts, and thus treat the parts as ultimately expendable. This does not earn them points in the human relations department, and the Ants in your company need to be balanced

W. MICHAEL (WOLFIE) DOOLEY

coyote

with other, more compassionate types. Ant works tirelessly, sacrificing herself with long hours to a job. Duty is, for her, not a grinding, resented task but an honorable path. "God is in the details," says Ant, becoming the craftsperson who finishes the backs of drawers, the unseen seams of lined clothing, the finish on the bottom of the tray, the careful buffing of machinery parts that will never be seen by another human eye, the calculating of data to many, many decimal points. For Ant, perfection is its own reward; Ant does not need or desire the pat on the head that keeps other types going. She simply does it because it needs to be done, and because it would be a betrayal of her nature to do it sloppily. Without the work of thousands of dogged, determined Ants, the well-oiled machinery of our civilization would grind to a chaotic halt.

coyote

Coyote is both the Fool and the Trickster; he is both innocent and obnoxious, sharp and gullible, occasionally wise and occasionally malicious. Coyotes are a recent arrival to the city; while their cousin wolf has been dying out through human encroachment, they have been adapting to the life of bandits, hiding in the hills or deserts or woods outside of cities and making nocturnal forays into them. Originally a denizen of the Southwest deserts, coyotes have spread throughout the entire continent; there is no continental American state that lacks them.

The most famous of all Coyote folk, of course, is Old Man Coyote himself—Whiskey Jack, the trickster god. Coyote can pull off magnificent tricks, and yet also pull amazing boners that backfire on him. He dies constantly in his myths, yet it is never a real death; more like that of a cartoon character, he bounces back and continues his trickster ways.

Coyote totem people are just as irrepressible, and treat death often with just as much disregard, as if it wasn't the same for them as for us other, ordinary mortals. To them, life is one big joke, and you and everyone else on the Earth is there to help them achieve their often hilarious aims. Coyote totem is a hard one to have, because it requires that they take on an archetype, living the role of the Trickster from day to day. As long as they are in their role, nothing can hurt them, but as soon as they leave it (which they will eventually have to do, being only human), the house of cards they have built may crash to the ground, leaving their mortal side to pick up the pieces. Coyote folk are excellent liars and deceivers, and love a tall tale and a good story. The best way to use the Coyote totem is to cajole Coyote into serving some cause. This is not Coyote's natural instinct, especially if it risks self-preservation, but Coyote energy can be fooled into it if you're clever, for a Coyote nature is as gullible as it is tricky. There will always be times when unfriendly outsiders threaten a group, and in some cases a bit of inspired lying is the only way to protect yourselves. This is what Coyote folk are for. They can sum up a situation with a glance, don a quick costume—which may only be a change of external attitude—and talk a line to fool the most unfriendly aggressor. In this way, they buy time while everyone else makes preparations, calls out reinforcements, or hides. Coyote dances a strange dance of his own making, and it makes him hard to get close to, unless you are sharp enough to follow him or else so trusting and loving that he couldn't ever bear to hurt you.

nineteen

Native Flora

THE URBAN HERBAL

• • Green things don't grow well in the city, especially plants. Trees live only a quarter of their normal lives due to air and ground pollution. Most of the rural wildflowers don't make it. Just like animals, however, some weeds and plants have adapted to the urban environment, and their stamina and endurance in the face of urban evolution can be magically utilized. These city weeds have magical properties that are different from those of their same-species rural counterparts.

Of course, the fact that there are fewer green spaces and more pollution in the city doesn't mean that the Green Man and the Earth Mother don't go there. They do, and they can be called upon, and they will answer; it just isn't their turf. Their centers of power lie elsewhere, but anywhere there is a patch of scrubby grass or a potted plant, they have a cosmic answering machine.

In the herbal that follows, we give only the magical and avoid the medicinal uses for each plant. If you want to know the medicinal uses, you can consult many good books on the subject. However, we need to put in a note of caution: City plants aren't necessarily good for your health. If they've spent a great deal of their lives less than fifty feet from a city street, they will have absorbed a lot of toxic chemicals from the exhaust of passing cars. Attempting to use them as medicine might make you even sicker than you are. Then again, if you're sick, poverty-stricken, adult size and weight, and have no other medical options, it might be worth the risk. Consult the spirits first.

For the magical uses, you need only pull and dry a bit of it and carry it with you, perhaps in a cloth bag or sachet or pressed in a book, checkbook, or wallet. Or you can make magical flower arrangements out of the fresh or dried plants. The petals of flowering plants can make magic mandalas when pressed onto a wet surface in circular designs. You can also make magical potpourri with several weeds in it, mixed with flower petals or standard potpourri to cover their scent.

"Reading the weeds" as you go through a neighborhood can give you an idea of the mental and emotional climate of the people who live there. Notice the clump of crabgrass here, the bunch of chicory there, and make an evaluation.

As it's good to be able to identify plants properly, get yourself a good guidebook to wild botany. Our favorite is actually a coloring book: *Common Weeds Coloring Book* by Stefen Bernath, from Dover Books. It has both black-and-white and color pictures of most of the plants listed below. Another good resource is the Peterson's Guides (to Wildflowers, to Medicinal Plants, and so on), which are specific to different areas of the country.

The Urban Herbal

Bindweed. Bindweed, or wild morning glory, is a rampant, twining weed that grows up anything it touches. It is used to keep a lover faithful—tie three knots in a sprig of it, unwound from some luckless plant. If it breaks, try again. If it breaks three times, it's a futile thing; that lover will never be faithful, no matter what, and you should give up trying.

Bittersweet. Bittersweet, or woody nightshade, is the slightly less poisonous cousin of belladonna. However, while the beautiful lady prefers a more rural area, bittersweet has made the cities her own. She resembles her cousin completely except that her berries are red instead of black. Like all nightshades, its charms are that of enchantment. This is dangerous magic to work with, and you must be careful not to tread on unethical pathways, but bittersweet can be given to a lover to strengthen their feelings for you. If it backfires, however, it will tend to be in the direction of unpleasant obsession, so be careful.

Burdock. Burdock is a plant of honesty. If you think someone is being dishonest with you, sneak the burrs onto their clothing. They will be forced to tell the truth, or dire consequences will result.

Butter-and-Eggs. Butter-and-eggs, or toadflax, is fairy food. Thus it acts not as food to fill the stomach, but as magic to convince the stomach that it is being filled. If you find yourself in a situation where you must refrain from eating, either voluntarily (dieting) or involuntarily (extreme poverty), carrying butter-and-eggs on your person will dull the hunger pangs and allow you to go that extra mile without physical sustenance.

Celandine. Celandine makes a yellow ink that works for magic spells regarding telling truth from falsehood, and placing a touch of it on one's glasses is said to eventually improve vision.

Chickweed. Chickweed, with its starry flowers like The Star in the Tarot deck, symbolizes hope. Give gifts of the dried leaves in magical potpourri to those who have lost hope and need her healing touch.

Chicory. With its bright blue flowers, chicory is cheerfulness. Bring it into the house to dispel negative energy after a fight or illness. Carry it in a pouch for depression.

Cinquefoil. Cinquefoil, or five-finger grass, is a magical amplifier. Adding it to any other spell jacks up the power. Since it resembles a certain other five-fingered plant, but is legal and innocuous, it can be used as a charm to distract the eyes of law enforcement away from use of said other plant. A bit of it can be dropped on the ground between you and watching eyes to temporarily turn them away.

Clover. Clover of any kind is the symbol of luck, and should be carried as such. Two-leaved ones are luck in relationships, three-leaved ones in money, and four-leaved ones in everything.

Crabgrass. One of the most hated weeds of all time, crabgrass can live anywhere, in any soil, and no matter how you pull it up, it comes back again. This is the magical plant to use for persistence, for telling someone (perhaps a dismissive politician or unfair bureaucrat) that you refuse to go away and, if you are obliterated, more rebels will crop up where you fall. Leave a root of crabgrass in his office, or on the threshold where he'll step over it, and he'll begin to take you seriously. Crabgrass is symbolic of the struggle for survival, and you can carry it (traditionally tucked into the laces of a shoe or boot) if your actual survival is in danger for some reason. The most magical part is the root, especially of a large clump; it resembles the crab for which it is named.

Dandelion. Symbol of the sun wherever it grows, and of brightness and courage. Its long roots don't come up easily, and when you pull it up, parts break off and grow again, keeping it indelibly in one place. Carry it for courage, and to keep from being evicted. Its coin-gold blossoms can also be gathered and put into a purse for a money spell. When the yellow flowers turn to white fluff, the sun gives way to the moon, and it can be used to teach small children the art of wish craft; have them wave or blow on them while making a wish.

Datura. The poisonous datura, or jimsonweed, is a banishing herb. Fling it at what you wish to get rid of. Don't keep it in your house except in a jar packed into a larger container in a layer or more of beneficent herbs to buffer its power.

Fruit Trees. All fruit trees—apple, crabapple, pear, et cetera—that actually bear fruit are symbolic of creativity, be it actual fertility (trying to get pregnant) or fertility of the mind. The flowering but non-fruiting types, on the other hand, can be used magically to bring beauty to a space, but their presence has a chilling effect on human reproduction.

Geranium. Geranium, often found potted on people's steps, is the keeping-up-with-the-Joneses plant. If you grow geraniums in your yard, your neighbors will all envy you, no matter how squalid your life. You won't be able to hide as easily, though, but for some people that's not as important.

Ginkgo. Ginkgo is another tree that is often planted ornamentally. Its leaves are carried for memory and clarity of mind.

Goldenrod. Goldenrod is a solar plant, and as such brings courage, self-confidence, warmth, wealth, and charisma. When paired with a lunar plant like moonseed, it symbolizes the union of opposites.

Ground Ivy. Ground ivy, also known as gill o' the ground, helps one overcome weakness and timidity if carried. Use it to lever yourself out of codependent relationships.

Hawthorn. Hawthorn doesn't grow wild in cities, but it is often planted deliberately in parks. It is one of the sacred ogham trees, dedicated to the dark side of the love goddess Aphrodite On The Tomb, the patron of all who kill themselves or another for love. It is a tree of terrible obsessions, wild passions, and dangerous emotions. Use the spike-like thorns in banishing bottle spells to give someone a terrible fear of going where you don't wish them to go. To stop someone who is committing violent crimes, stab hawthorns through an animal heart (chicken is okay; you can get animal hearts at the butcher shop or at ethnic supermarkets), bind it up with black thread, and bury it or throw it down a storm drain.

Hosta. Hosta, which is not a wild herb but a domestic plant very popular in the front beds of commercial establishments, makes one able to pass unnoticed. Carry a leaf of it and it will do the trick. It is not exactly an invisibility spell; you will be seen, but no one will take any notice of you. You will become an ultimately unimportant detail to be ignored as assiduously as possible. This, of course, is why it is a bad idea for commercial establishments, but of course you can't tell them anything—we're only witches, what do we know?

Ivy. Ivy is a general all-purpose guard against ill fortune. One of the sacred ogham plants, a sprig of it can be carried for good luck, or a wreath of it woven for passion. Like the grapevine, it is sacred to Dionysus, and having too much ivy can lead to excess, overconfidence, and risky behavior.

Knotgrass. Knotgrass is a good protection plant to use if you want to keep intruders away from a particular place. Leave it at the threshold or path entrance, somewhere they'd be likely to approach, and it will turn them away by making things suddenly difficult with some kind of distraction.

Kudzu. Kudzu, the creeping plant that has taken over much of the South, is symbolic of alcoholism and drug addiction. To break such a habit, twine it into a wreath and throw it from a high place, such as a tall building. Make sure that you do not step over it when you leave the building, so that it won't try to "stick" to you again.

Maple. Maple trees symbolize the love of family for each other. Planting one in the yard or on the sidewalk strengthens familial bonds. Bringing a branch into the house does the trick too, for a shorter period of time. The leaves can be used in charms to protect children and keep them safe.

Milkweed. Milkweed is good for bringing good energy into a house or apartment, and clearing out the tense energy. Cut stalks of it and bring it inside; set it in vases by the door.

Moonseed. Moonseed is a lunar plant, symbolizing intuition, emotions, nurturing, and the feminine cycle. When paired with a solar plant like goldenrod, they symbolize the union of opposites.

Mullein. Mullein is a multipurpose plant. It wards and guards; drives off depression; clears the chest of coughs, if smoked or drunk in a tea; can be dipped in wax or liquor and used as a torch; and wards off nightmares when placed under your pillow.

Oaks. Oak trees, often planted in cities, are the ultimate plant symbol of strength. Carrying oak leaves refreshes and buoys you up; weaving a wreath of them and wearing it every night for ten minutes while saying "NO!" will help you set strong boundaries and stick to them.

Ornamental Kale. Ornamental kale, often seen planted around stores, is a money-drawer. It gives one sales ability, and helps merchandise to pass. Useful for stores and small businesses, and for anyone going for a job interview.

Peppergrass. Peppergrass, or poor man's pepper, is used in spells for wealth; crumble its seeds and carry them in a small pouch with a few coins. It can also be used in bottle spells.

Petunias. Petunias, often grown domestically in the city in planters, promote cheer and cut down on confrontation. They have a rather brainless, happy vibe to them, but sometimes that's just the right antidote to inner-city hostility.

Pine. Pine trees belong to the Green Man, no matter where they are. Pine trees are especially good conduits to whatever's left of the earth energy below the concrete. Hug one to gain strength. When moving through the more commercial districts of the city, the form one most often finds pine in is pine bark mulch, layered thickly around shrubs. If you're feeling fatigue, take some and crumble it in your hand. When it's powdered enough, take off your shoes and sprinkle some into them, then put them back on. Pine will give you the strength to walk another mile.

Pineappleweed. Used for enhancing psychic powers. Put a sprig under your pillow at night in order to have prophetic dreams.

Plantain. Plantain, also known as waybread, is the traveler's friend. Its seeds were once ground to make an edible flour that would sustain hungry wanderers, and so it is a good charm to carry for those who are without a regular address or just passing through and need to be sustained psychically lest they fall into depression. Shield-shaped, it is also a protective plant, making a wayfarer invisible to potential harm.

Pokeberry. The juice of its berries are used to make ink, so pokeberry is symbolic of learning and information, a well to dip into. Don't eat the berries (mild poison), but carry them in a mojo bag to find the knowledge you seek.

Poplar. Poplar trees are often found in civic plantings. It is a money tree and the buds are used in money spells.

Prickly lettuce. Prickly lettuce helps one recover from sudden trauma and long-term agony. Dry and crush the leaves, and burn them in an incense; breathe this and you will feel healed and renewed.

Purslane. Purslane symbolizes fresh, robust health. It is full of vitamin C and can be nibbled on as a snack. Growing it around your yard guarantees the health of those therein.

Queen Anne's lace. Queen Anne's lace, or wild carrot, has an edible root and leaves that make a nice tea. Its blossoms, when dried and crushed, are a spell for good hostessing. Scattered throughout the house, they make a party pleasant and not chaotic; those whose job is making people feel welcome, such as maitre d's, should carry the blossoms on their person.

Ragweed. Ragweed bestows the quality that the Romans called *audacia* and that is referred to in Yiddish as *chutzpah*. It is the ability to stand up and spit in the eye of an opponent that is sure to crush you, whether or not you can possibly win. Ragweed is in-your-face and refuses to leave; its jagged pollen crystals get into your bronchial tubes and won't leave you alone. It will give you desperate self-confidence in desperate situations.

Roses. Roses, which grow in city yards and gardens all over the country, are sacred to the love goddess, and all symbolize love. The wilder the rose variety, the more wild and intense the love. Red is for sexual passion, pink for affection, peach or orange for mother-child love, white for grandparents and respected elders, lavender for long-term marriages, and yellow for friendship.

Rowan. Rowan is sometimes planted on city streets. It is a tree of great protection, one of the sacred ogham trees. The orange-red berries that it bears in the autumn will ward off just about any malevolent influence that can be warded off.

Sandburr. Sandburr, or sandspur, is a plant of sorrow. To rid yourself of sorrow, pluck some of it and leave it as an offering on a gravestone in a cemetery.

Shepherd's Purse. The heart-shaped leaves of shepherd's purse show that it is a plant of love, and can be used to bring a new love into your life or strengthen an old one. It is sacred to the goddess, and can be used as an offering to her, especially in her aspects as a deity of love and affection.

Staghorn Sumac. Like its name implies, staghorn sumac is sacred to the Horned Hunter, and its presence offers protection from those being hunted for any reason. It can also be used as an offering to the God. Its bark, brewed, makes a lemonade-like tea.

Tumbleweed. Carrying a tumbleweed in the trunk of your car is said to get you those extra few miles home when the car is threatening to break down. It will hold everything together until you get somewhere safe enough to fall apart.

Virginia Creeper. Virginia creeper, a Southern pest plant, is used to ward off insecurity and other creeping, dark thoughts. Pull it up and tie it in knots, and burn or bury it or throw it down a storm drain.

Willow. Willow is a feminine, sacred, lunar tree, one of the sacred ogham trees. It symbolizes changeability, and is often planted in parks. If someone has a rigid, inflexible attitude toward life, weave a wreath of willow withes for them and hide it in their home or office or car. They will begin to bend and learn flexibility.

Wood Sorrel. For all its rural name, wood sorrel is often found in the wilder areas of cities. It symbolizes innocence, and can be used in charms to protect children.

Conclusion

Five years ago, Raven escaped the city after a long imprisonment there. He had learned many of its secrets, but he was commanded by his Goddess to go elsewhere and live another life. He still comes into the city at certain times of the year when the trashpicking is really good, however, and he does not forget his time there. Tannin, on the other hand, is so thoroughly enmeshed with her city that it is unlikely that she will ever leave it. She'll be there in ten or twenty years, still talking to the spirit of Worcester and checking the sidewalks for omens.

That's one of the things that we found most valuable in our collaboration on this book. Half of the people living in the city right now love it and would never leave, except perhaps for another city. The other half hate it, and are biding their time and saving their money—or living lives of quiet despair. But ignorance is helplessness, and even if you don't like it there, knowledge of its secrets and motions, its gifts and pitfalls and mysteries, will give you that extra boost to keep going each morning.

In long-ago days, peasants lived in small villages, islands of safety so distant from each other that they might go their entire lives seeing no other place. These islands were often separated by wild forest, filled with deadly animals and deadlier brigands. Similarly, some city dwellers, especially the ones who aren't thrilled about being there, may crouch fearfully in their apartments or neighborhoods as if they were islands of safety in the midst of danger, and in the process miss out on a great many interesting and useful things.

Although there are still rural poor in some areas of this country, the poverty-stricken are, increasingly, moving to urban areas. There have always been poor people in cities, but it seems now as if the majority of the "folk," the "people," the "peasants"—and before you take offense to that term, remember that it was the peasants who held on to the old religions the longest, for whom the very word *pagan* was coined—are now an urban population. If this is the case, it's not surprising that the cities are where the new Paganism, the new lore of the people, is springing up. We can only hope that we, as modern Pagans, are flexible enough to recognize urban Paganism as a legitimate adaptation to our current living habits, and one which will not fade away soon.

Suggested Reading

Arnold, Charles. *Ritual Body Art: Drawing the Spirit.* Custer, Wash.: Phoenix Publishing Co., 1997.

(This is a great book on using non-permanent body art for serious ritual.)

Bonewits, Issac. *Real Magic.* York Beach, Maine: Samuel Weiser, 1993.

(An entertaining perspective on modern magic, Paganism, and the Kitchen Sink.)

Cunningham, Scott. *Cunningham's Encyclopedia of Crystal, Gem and Metal Magic.* St. Paul, Minn.: Llewellyn Publications, 1995.

(This is an easy-to-follow guide to all sorts of crystals and minerals.)

———. *Encyclopedia of Magical Herbs.* St. Paul, Minn.: Llewellyn Publications, 1985.

(Supplement to Native Flora chapter.)

Ferrar, Janet, and Stewart Ferrar. *Spells and How They Work.* Custer, Wash.: Phoenix Publishing Co., 1990.

(All you wanted to know about casting spells but were afraid to ask.)

———. *The Witches' God: The Masculine Principle of Divinity.* Custer, Wash.: Phoenix Publishing Co., 1991.

(A quick and dirty guide to male world deities. It has a great bibliography.)

———. *The Witches' Goddess: The Feminine Principle of Divinity.* Custer, Wash.: Phoenix Publishing Co., 1989.
(A quick and dirty guide to female world deities. It has a great bibliography.)

Fortune, Dion. *Psychic Self-Defense.* Boston: Red Wheel, 2001.
(The mother of all psychic defense books.)

González-Wippler, Migene. *Santería: The Religion, Faith, Rites, Magic.* St. Paul, Minn.: Llewellyn Publications, 1994.
(This is a simple primer on Santería.)

Kowalchik, Claire, and William H. Hylton. *Rodale's Illustrated Encyclopedia of Herbs.* Emmaus, Pa.: Rodale Press, 1987.
(This is a non-magical guide to herbs. It is very accurate, and talks about the dangers as well as benefits of working with the plants therein.)

Morgan, Keith. *Crystal Magick.* London: Pentacle Enterprises, 1992.
(This is a good book that goes into selecting stones and working with them.)

Rushkoff, Douglas. *Cyberia: Life in the Trenches of Cyberspace.* New York, N.Y.: Harper Collins, 1995.
(This book is supplemental to chapter 16, Spirit in the Wires. Not an easy read, but very spiritual and poetic. Written by someone who understands both computer technology and shamanism. NOT AN EASY OR QUICK READ. An absolute must to computer-oriented Chaos magicians!)

Teish, Luisah. *Carnival of the Spirit: Seasonal Celebrations and Rites of Passage.* San Francisco, Calif.: Harper, 1994.
(This is a good beginner's guide to Voodoo.)

Telesco, Patricia, and Sirona Knight. *The Wiccan Web.* Sacramento, Calif.: Citadel Press, 2001.

(This is a supplemental book to chapter 16.)

Wilson, Robert Anton. *Prometheus Rising.* Tempe, Arizona: New Falcon Publications, 1986.

(This book is about the essence of magic without any cosmic clutter. Geek out with Bob Wilson if you have the time—he's the cat's pajamas.)

INDEX

REACH FOR THE MOON

Llewellyn publishes hundreds of books on your favorite subjects!
To get these exciting books, including the ones on the following pages, check your local bookstore or order them directly from Llewellyn.

Order by Phone

- Call toll-free within the U.S. and Canada, 1-877-NEW WRLD
- In Minnesota, call (651) 291-1970
- We accept VISA, MasterCard, and American Express

Order by Mail

- Send the full price of your order (MN residents add 7% sales tax) in U.S. funds, plus postage & handling to:

  Llewellyn Worldwide
  P.O. Box 64383, Dept. 0-7387-0259-5
  St. Paul, MN 55164–0383, U.S.A.

Postage & Handling

- **Standard** (U.S., Mexico, & Canada) If your order is:
  $20 or under, add $5
  $20.01–$100, add $6
  Over $100, shipping is free

(Continental U.S. orders ship UPS. AK, HI, PR, & P.O. Boxes ship USPS 1st class. Mex. & Can. ship PMB.)

- **Second Day Air** (Continental U.S. only): $10 for one book plus $1 per each additional book
- **Express** (AK, HI, & PR only) [Not available for P.O. Box delivery. For street address delivery only.]: $15 for one book plus $1 per each additional book
- **International Surface Mail:** $20 or under, add $5 plus $1 per item; $20.01 and over, add $6 plus $1 per item
- **International Airmail:** Books—Add the retail price of each item; Non-book items—Add $5 per item

Please allow 4–6 weeks for delivery on all orders.
Postage and handling rates subject to change.

Discounts

We offer a 20% discount to group leaders or agents. You must order a minimum of 5 copies of the same book to get our special quantity price.

FREE CATALOG

Get a free copy of our color catalog, *New Worlds of Mind and Spirit*. Subscribe for just $10.00 in the United States and Canada ($30.00 overseas, airmail). Call 1-877-NEW WRLD today!

Visit our website at www.llewellyn.com for more information.

NOCTURNAL WITCHCRAFT

Magick After Dark

Konstantinos

The promise of dark delights.

Nightkind, goths, children of the night . . . by whichever name you call them, they represent a major force in the New Age world. They are seekers intrigued by the mysteries of the occult and Witchcraft, yet disappointed by books that equate dark mysteries with evil.

This book delivers a unique experience, beginning with an explanation of why some are drawn to the night and the aspects of deity that represent the dark, followed by powers and rituals available under the cover of shadow. From divining with the night to reading minds, from enhancing personal magnetism to altering reality, *Nocturnal Witchcraft* fulfills the esoteric needs of anyone who appreciates dark mystique.

- Unveils a system of magic that will appeal to a neglected and often misunderstood audience searching for positive expression.
- Presents the dark aspects of magic in a positive way, dispelling the myths that light is always good and dark is always evil.

0-7387-0166-1

288 pp., 6 x 9, appendices **$14.95**

SACRED GEOMETRY ORACLE

Become the Architect of Your Life

John Michael Greer

Use the same tools that designed temples and pyramids to design your own life.

From the time of Stonehenge and the Pyramids, through the mystical teachings of Pythagoras to the cutting edge of advanced science, the cosmic patterns and universal truths of sacred geometry bridge past and future. Now, for the first time, you can put this ancient wisdom to work in your own life with the *Sacred Geometry Oracle.*

This kit contains thirty-three cards, each representing a basic figure in traditional sacred geometry, and each relating to one of the basic patterns of the universe—patterns that form the hidden structure of our everyday lives. Use the cards for divination, meditation, and self-exploration.

- The only divination system that draws on the traditions of sacred geometry.
- The book *Techniques for Geometric Transformation* presents the meanings of each card, how to cast and interpret readings with several original layouts, and meditations.
- Provides clear, insightful, and accurate readings about past, present, and future events.
- A tool for expanding awareness of the patterns of reality that shape our lives.

0-7387-0051-7
Boxed kit: 33-card deck and 6 x 9, 240-pp. illustrated guidebook **$34.95**

To order, call 1-877-NEW WRLD

Prices subject to change without notice

To Write to the Authors

If you wish to contact the authors or would like more information about this book, please write to the authors in care of Llewellyn Worldwide and we will forward your request. Both the authors and publisher appreciate hearing from you and learning of your enjoyment of this book and how it has helped you. Llewellyn Worldwide cannot guarantee that every letter written to the authors can be answered, but all will be forwarded. Please write to:

Raven Kaldera & Tannin Schwartzstein
℅ Llewellyn Worldwide
P.O. Box 64383, Dept. 0-7387-0259-5
St. Paul, MN 55164-0383, U.S.A.

Please enclose a self-addressed stamped envelope for reply, or $1.00 to cover costs. If outside U.S.A., enclose international postal reply coupon.

Many of Llewellyn's authors have websites with additional information and resources. For more information, please visit our website at:

http://www.llewellyn.com